THE HALO EFFECT

How

# VOLUNTEERING

CAN LEAD TO A

MORE FULFILLING LIFE

—AND A

BETTER CAREER

## JOHN RAYNOLDS
WITH GENE STONE

Golden Books
NEW YORK

*Golden Books*®

888 Seventh Avenue
New York, NY 10106

Designed by Gwen Petruska Gürkan


Manufactured in the United States of America


10 9 8 7 6 5 4 3 2 1

Library of Congress Cataloging-in-Publication Data

Raynolds, John.
The halo effect : how volunteering can lead to a more
fulfilling life—and a better career / John Raynolds with Gene
Stone.
p.     cm.
ISBN 0-307-44071-0 (alk. paper)
1. Voluntarism—United States.   2. Volunteers—United States.
3. Career changes—United States.   I. Stone, Gene W.   II. Title.
HN90.V64R388      1998
361.3'7—dc21                                    98-7098
                                                    CIP

To the millions of men and women who find time to balance the demands of their jobs with the joy of volunteer service.

And above all to my wife, Eileen, who, as she rose to become president of a large corporation, always made time to help others, and reached out to me in a time of great personal tragedy and taught me that life is good and the human spirit resilient.

# CONTENTS

THE HALO EFFECT

# WHAT IS THE HALO EFFECT?

The word "halo" has several meanings. It was first used in a business context in the 1930s, in AT&T's landmark study of the effects of working conditions on productivity.

In the study, assembly-plant working conditions were dramatically improved through better lighting, ventilation, more efficient workstation seating, and so forth. The company found that as a result of these innovations, productivity increased significantly.

Then the research team decided to see if the converse was true—did poorer conditions reduce productivity? And so they reduced the plant's lighting, air flow, and so on.

The result was surprising: Instead of dropping, productivity levels remained significantly higher than normal. It turned out that the workers were reacting positively to the attentive efforts of the research team monitoring them, regardless of the actual conditions surrounding them. This result became known as the "halo effect."

"Halo" has other meanings. In the military, HALO can mean High Altitude Low Opening, referring to a parachute jump in which the paratrooper exits the plane at high altitude, but waits an agonizing time before opening the chute close to the ground to avoid detection. In religion, the halo is a luminous ring seen around the heads or bodies of sacred beings that represents holiness or saintliness. In meteorology, it's a band of colored light surrounding a light source, such as the sun or moon, caused by the refraction and reflection of light by suspended ice particles.

But in this book, the halo effect describes the unplanned side benefits to your career that so often occur when you reach out to help others.

You will soon read the stories of many people for whom the halo effect became a wonderful reality. Not only did giving make them feel better about themselves, but their careers took unexpected, positive turns for the better. This fallout from good works is not something that anyone can plan, but it happens, time after time. After you've learned how the halo effect has impacted the lives of others, and you've taken a look at your own interests and personality and had a chance to assess them against the myriad skills and attributes needed by not-for-profit organizations, you'll be ready to select one of the paths to volunteer service listed in the appendix—or, perhaps, to find another path of your own.

Don't expect your halo to shine immediately. However, the good feelings you'll get from helping will start right away. You'll find you're gaining more from your good works than you're investing. This psychic income, the feelings of joy and satisfaction always reported by those serving others, will far outweigh the time and energy you devote to volunteering.

And yes, at some point the halo effect *will* impact your career—perhaps when you least expect it. For instance, at age sixty-eight, I've recently taken on a new job, as president and chief executive officer of the National Peace Garden Monument. My mission is to expand its board of directors and to raise the money needed to commence the monument's construction. I'm truly energized and passionate about this shining new opportunity. What a wonderful way to cap a career—and to do something positive and lasting for peace. Best of all, this job came to me unbeckoned, through the halo effect, a direct result of some pro bono consulting work I'd done more than a year ago for the National Executive Service Corps, helping them with their planning and succession process. In these pages, I'll trace the path that led me here (and also recount the inspiring story of Elizabeth Ratcliff, who worked for eleven years to bring this project to reality).

Remember, when you become involved, when you lead with your heart as well as your head, the result is always good. And given the halo effect that we know is out there, you'll not only become a better person, but your career will also benefit in wonderful and unexpected ways.

## PART I

# GOOD WORKS

*Goodness is the only investment that never fails.*

Henry David Thoreau

Last year, just before Christmas, a young man in trouble showed up at my door. Scott was the son of a close friend. Shyly, he sat down in the living room, downed a beer in a few quick gulps, and told me, without any feeling, that he was lost.

He hardly looked it. An attractive, soft-spoken man in his early thirties, Scott made a good living as a midlevel manager at a large software company where he'd worked since graduating from college. He had majored in mathematics and computer science, and his education had been precisely designed to prepare him for his current job.

He admitted almost with shame that his personal life was also what he'd hoped for and expected. He'd married a woman he'd met on a European vacation. She had been with someone else at the time, as had he, but the two of them felt an instant connection and married a year later. They argued once a week, and made up almost immediately thereafter. They had four in-laws, three children, two cars, one dog, and enough money in the bank.

It was a good life, Scott said. "At least," he added, "good enough"—which seemed to mean that he thought it *wasn't* good enough.

I asked him if he could talk more about his emotions, but he told me outright that he couldn't. He had few words on the subject, and frankly, he thought he had already used them up.

We talked about other things for a while—politics, sports, family—and then we slowly returned to the topic of Scott's despondency.

"I guess it's work," he said. "My home life is good. My job just isn't."

Now that he had opened the door to what was really bothering him, he couldn't stop talking. It was as though, once he had admitted to having a problem, he had to make sure I understood it.

His work itself was interesting, he said. What was driving him crazy was that there were dozens of other managers in similar positions all vying for the few slots open above them. He didn't feel he could compete. He could sense that his supervisors were waiting for him to impress them, but beyond being diligent and capable, he couldn't think of any other way to shine.

"Every one of us is basically the same person," he said, "How do I find a way to stand out?"

I didn't say anything, because I sensed that Scott hadn't finished talking. He hadn't.

"Furthermore," he said, "I'm kind of bored with my job. I've been doing it for ten years, and I'm good. But I'd love to see what else I can do in life."

I started to speak. Scott interrupted. For a man of few words, tonight he had quite a few at his disposal. "There must be other things I can do. But I can't take any risks at work now. Not with everything being so tense."

He paused for a moment. A little more aware of his speech patterns, I waited for him to continue.

He did. "I don't have any right to complain," he said. "There are many others out there who don't have what I have."

But it was clear to me, as well as to him, that he was complaining, that he had no real talent for the job, and that he didn't want to do it. He was unhappy, and sometimes unhappiness can happen even to the happiest of people.

Scott went on for a while: he needed to stretch himself more, he wanted to meet people outside his business. Was there anything wrong, he finally asked, in feeling this way?

"I doubt it," I said.

"Then what am I doing wrong?" he asked.

"You're probably not doing anything wrong," I said. "Maybe it's just that there are other things you could be doing, too."

Since Scott knew my background fairly well, he tried to guess what I had in mind.

"An Outward Bound trip?" he asked. His father had met me when I was CEO of the outdoors-oriented program. "I don't think that would help. Anyway, I'm not an outside kind of guy."

"I wasn't thinking of Outward Bound," I said. "Have you ever thought about what I like to call the halo effect?"

"The halo effect?" he asked.

I explained to him what I meant by the phrase: Whenever you volunteer your time and your energy, whether it's helping a disabled runner to participate in a marathon, or serving dinner at a homeless shelter, or caring for someone suffering from AIDS, you're doing more than assisting another human being. Indirectly, you're helping yourself, too. The warm glow from that effort somehow manages to find its way back into your own life.

"I can understand why all this might be good for my soul," Scott admitted. "But right now, it's my job that's driving me crazy."

"The halo effect doesn't just affect your soul," I said. "It touches your career, too."

"How?" Scott asked.

The answer to Scott's question is the subject of this book. Volunteerism, or good works, or public service, or the third sector (the first two sectors being the public and private)—whatever you want to call it, it's good for you, and it's good for your career.

## KATHY LEBLANC'S STORY

I spent most of my career working in middle management at a Fortune 500 company. I earned a good living, but when I remarried, it wasn't necessary for me to work anymore. So I didn't.

Well, that lasted about six weeks. I couldn't stand sitting at home. But I wasn't sure what to do, so when a friend told me she was volunteering at the Audubon Zoo in New Orleans, I decided to come along—I'd grown up near the zoo and had always liked it. I went through the zoo's volunteer-training program, and fell in love with the work.

I started out as what they call an "edzoocator" and also worked on the zoo-mobile, which goes out to the ill and the infirm. And since I had computer experience, I started assisting the volunteer coordinator in automating her program. Seven months later the coordinator resigned, and I applied for the position and got it. Today I manage the entire volunteer program. It's like running a personnel office for unpaid staff.

All in all, it's the best job in the world. I love animals. At home I have three dogs, two cats, and a rabbit. Here I've developed a crush on the Sumatran tigers; I say hello to them every day. I can't believe I'm getting paid for something I once volunteered to do.

The notion of volunteer work is hardly new, and certainly not in America, which has long possessed a tradition of helping hands. From the earliest colonial days, settlers helped one another clear forested land, build log houses, and harvest crops. In the absence of doctors and trained midwives, they guided one another in illness and childbirth. Public protection was guaranteed by freely made associations of townspeople. Model citizens set a standard for volunteerism; they included Benjamin Franklin, who helped create a library, the first volunteer fire department, the University of Pennsylvania, and the American Philosophical Society.

Other great Americans continued the volunteer tradition, perhaps none surpassing Jane Addams, whose Chicago-based Hull House became one of the country's most influential social-service providers, setting a standard for intelligent interaction between volunteer and recipient.

During this time, Americans in want looked to one another rather than to government for aid. Money for organizational efforts also came from citizens: The late 1800s were marked by the emergence of some of the greatest philanthropists in history, including Andrew Carnegie; John D. Rockefeller, who gave away $531 million in his lifetime; and Henry Ford, whose foundation still contributes more than $100 million each year.

This citizen-driven situation changed during and after the Depression, however, as then-overwhelming societal needs were met increasingly by government agencies and institutions. Programs for the poor, the unemployed, the aged, and the ill were formed and quickly burgeoned, including the first Social Security legislation, passed in 1935.

Government programs received another shot in the arm during the administration of Lyndon B. Johnson, with the introduction of his Great Society and the War on Poverty. Medicare was established to provide free medical care to the aged. Federal aid for education at all levels was greatly expanded. Antipoverty programs were funded with federal money. The Department of Housing and Urban Development was created.

All things change. Today the United States is facing another shift as the pendulum swings back toward spending less federal money for social programs. Faith in our government's ability to solve, or even ameliorate, social problems has sunk to a low level. Citizens no longer have confidence that Congress will do what's right. As a result, Americans in need can no longer count on the government to provide a security net.

Something else has changed in this country.

Since World War II, Americans have gone on a binge of acquiring and owning: houses, vacation homes, cars, appliances, technology. This acquisitiveness is understandable in the context of wartime shortages and sacrifice, and the American Dream was and is a commendable one: Work hard, own your own home, have a yard, tend a garden, raise a family, and give them all everything you can.

But despite the great successes of our country, the last fifty years have taken a toll on the national spirit.

For one thing, amid all that buying and spending, less tangible values were ignored. Church attendance has dropped, and spirituality's relevance has diminished. Climbing the job ladder has become paramount. Families have become portable, and communities turned into fluid places of temporary residence. Rather than living a lifetime in one house or apartment, Americans now move every five years.

Prosperity, our overriding goal, has become a two-tiered phenomenon, with the emergence of a successful upper middle class matched by the rapid growth of an impoverished underclass. Drug use has become a national epidemic, and crime of all varieties has risen dramatically.

And, as the increased globalization of business in the 1980s exposed the need to streamline operations for competitiveness and productivity, we have seen dramatic changes in the workplace. The explosive development of computer technology has allowed whole layers of middle management to be peeled away. After twenty or twenty-five years of service at an IBM, an Eastman Kodak, an AT&T, good people are being told that they are no longer needed. An article of faith has been broken. People now ask themselves, "Will my department be eliminated next?"

During this same period of downsizing, government has grown exorbitantly and, as a nation, we have run up large debts for our children to pay. Young people are dropping out of schools whose curricula don't seem relevant and, despite the vast sums spent, we can't get a handle on controlling drugs and crime.

The American picture is not all dark. In the nineties, we have regained our competitive position in global markets and are now the world's most efficient industrialized nation. We stayed the course in the Cold War and emerged the unchallenged world leader.

Yet millions of Americans feel a void inside. They lack a sense of wholeness. They are anxious about their jobs, or if they have sufficient resources, they wonder, as Peggy Lee once sang, "Is that all there is?" They want more than material goods and big bank accounts. They want to feel fulfilled emotionally and spiritually.

## MARY HOLDRIDGE'S STORY

When I was in college I'd thought about a career in radio, but my school's station offered few chances for students to get involved. So I drifted into film instead; after graduating I came to California and got a job in rock videos, and that led to other positions until I landed a job working for a major film producer, starting off as office runner and going on to become director of development. I worked there for about six years, and although I liked my bosses, I didn't care much for the film business.

So I started doing volunteer work. I'd done it before, but I never found anything particularly satisfying. Then one of my bosses started a wonderful program called Camp Pacific Heartland, which is a summer camp for kids with AIDS or HIV, or whose parents or loved ones are living with it or have passed away.

The kids range from five to eighteen years old, and they have a great time, because they're able to hang out with other kids in a similar situation. The sad fact is there's still an enormous stigma about the disease, and these kids can't always find someone who understands what they're going through.

The camp lets them do what any camp would: They play games and sports, they make crafts, and so on. And since we're in Los Angeles, sometimes celebrities visit, and that really makes the kids happy. Above all, the kids come to camp to have fun.

At the camp I met another volunteer who had landed a job at a local public radio station, producing a show called "Morning Becomes Eclectic." After she got there she heard about a job in the fundraising department, and she told them about me. They called me in, and I got the job. I started in late 1996.

I still do fundraising, which is pretty essential in public radio, but now I also produce a program called "The Treatment," which is a film and culture interview show. It's just what I wanted.

It's funny—not long ago my parents moved to a new house and among all the scattered boxes and cartons I found a copy of my college entrance essay. It was about how some day I wanted to be the program director for an alternative radio station.

Let's take another look at the major trends mentioned above. There is a significant change in the way our government handles the problems of the impoverished, the disabled, and the underprivileged; moreover, there is a sense of inner emptiness among our citizens.

Now let's merge these two issues. The slack created by the government can be taken up by people like you. The work of federal agencies can increasingly be handled by private citizens. This is a point that has been made by countless leaders of the nonprofit community. Help others, and you help your country as well as yourself. You quiet that anxious voice within.

Volunteerism can help your country and it can soothe your soul. These are both significant motives for getting involved.

But there's yet another personal benefit to volunteerism, or what I like to call good works, that is seldom discussed but nonetheless tangible, often immediate, and always powerful.

What is that benefit?

A boost to your career.

Over the last few years I've given many lectures across the country. I've discovered a startling number of people like Scott: both men and women, ranging in age from their twenties to their fifties or beyond, all of them with solid careers or career possibilities, but all of them feeling unfulfilled and uninspired. Their chosen career hasn't been as promising as they'd have liked, and the solutions they've been offered—to stay at the office longer, or to compete more aggressively—haven't worked for them.

I often tell these people about my own professional life, a patchwork of different positions. I didn't just change jobs along the way; I changed careers, moving from investment banking to heavy manufacturing, from selling cars to government service, and so on. All of these situations were challenging, but I can't say that any one of them could have kept me occupied, or even interested, for a lifetime. Although in the long run I can look back at a fulfilling career, I certainly had my share of times during those years when I felt as stuck as my friend Scott.

There was, however, one single thread that always held everything else together: No matter what I was doing, where I lived, or for whom I worked,

I always performed volunteer work for someone, somehow. I did that solely because I wanted to. Causes of various sorts have always meant a great deal to me, whether it's helping young people start a career, or raising money for a church, or working with the disabled. Over the years I've worked in ten separate careers and have served on the board of over twenty not-for-profit organizations.

But the startling part of this story, I tell people, is that my volunteer work has consistently given back to me more than I ever gave, although that was never my motivation—in fact, it's something I didn't even realize until many years later. But my career simply would not have been as successful if I hadn't struggled to do the right thing whenever I could.

For instance, after I graduated from Williams College in the early 1950s, I was accepted into the Vick Chemical Company marketing trainee program, and soon went to work. This happened concurrent with the Korean War, and since I felt the need to serve my country, I volunteered for the Navy and was shipped off to Korea, where I worked in underwater demolition. Vicks discontinued my salary while I was in the service, but they continued to send me holiday checks and other annual bonuses.

After leaving the Navy, I wanted to live in California, so I decided to attend Stanford University's business school, which had a strong West Coast alumni group. Then I thought about all the checks Vicks had sent me during the war. I'd only worked for the company a few months, and I had no intention of going back. The right thing to do was to return the money. So I did.

Vicks wrote back, saying that they refused to cash my check because I had served our country, and they had wanted to show their appreciation.

This was an early lesson that doing the right thing can have unexpected rewards. Returning the money was important to me, but when Vicks refused to keep it, not only did I feel good, *they* felt good, too.

Throughout my career, earning money has never been my primary goal. When I left my first business (selling cars in Salinas, California) to enter government service in Africa, I took an 80 percent cut in pay. This was in 1961, when the Cold War was at its coldest. I had just heard President Kennedy proclaiming that we should ask ourselves what we could do for our country; I felt that after almost a decade of making money, it was once more time to serve.

That pay cut was difficult for my family, but as luck would have it, the contacts I made during my government service eventually led to my next job as the factory personnel manager for M&M candies, which not only paid handsomely, but was a wonderful position for anyone with three young children. They ran to school to tell their classmates that their Dad ran a candy factory.

My work at M&M helped me find a mentor—an important part of volunteerism, as you'll see. When my mentor moved up the corporate side of the Mars organization, he asked me to come with him to Washington to help him acquire companies for the Mars organization.

That job was quite interesting, but eventually I grew restless and left the business, even though I still had a family to support. I've always felt that life is too short to spend time doing something you don't like.

Through a contact from my undergraduate days at Williams College I landed in investment banking, which I enjoyed, and which led to still another career through one of my corporate clients: They offered me the presidency of one of their divisions. Once more, a career change.

During this period I was looking for other ways to fulfill myself and became involved in not-for-profit service again by serving on the board of Outward Bound USA, probably the most satisfying not-for-profit work I've ever done. Then, after nine years, Outward Bound's board asked me to apply for the job of CEO of the organization.

I was thrilled, but the board selected someone else, thrusting me into a deep depression. However, that man turned the job down, and the board came back to me. Being second choice didn't bother me at all; considering my interest in the outdoors and in service, this was the job of my dreams. And it stayed that way throughout my nine-year tenure.

After working at Outward Bound I went off on my own to start a consulting business. Soon afterward, my wife, Ellie, died in a tragic accident, and I struggled, trying to cope with her death. Rather than run my own business, I decided to join Ward Howell, the world's seventh-largest executive recruitment firm. Not long after that I ran for election as the company's CEO, got the job, and stayed there almost four years.

I had known the people at Ward Howell in part because Ellie had worked there, and also through Outward Bound; I'd once given a team-building speech to Ward Howell partners at their annual convention. They knew my role in the not-for-profit world, and they liked my Outward Bound background and the values it represented. This connection, they told me, was the reason they gave me the top job.

The thrust of this eclectic career has not been to make me a remarkably wealthy man, but the money was always sufficient, and I've always felt good about the things I've done. And I have learned a couple of lessons. First, whenever you do the right thing, you feel better about yourself. And when you feel good, you tend to be more successful. You throw yourself into your work with more enthusiasm and energy, particularly if you are aligned with the values of the company. You relate better to other people, too, for a good attitude is contagious.

I also learned, during those troubled times when my career needed a boost, that such a helping hand more often than not appeared from someone or something connected to my volunteer work rather than my professional experience. It came from people I had met, from skills I had developed, from risks I had taken in the not-for-profit world. Again, I didn't always realize this at the time, but that's one of the great advantages of age: being able to look back and see patterns that are impossible to spot while you're living them.

As we talk more about the specific ways in which volunteerism helps to create a good career, you'll see that it wasn't the right solution only for me; it's right for anyone who, just like my friend Scott, is thinking, "I'm unhappy at work and in my life. How can I feel better about my job, improve my career, and make more money?"

The answer is: Help someone else. Enter the not-for-profit sector. It's good for your soul. It's good for your business.

# JEFFREY SMART'S STORY

I grew up in West Virginia; then, after getting a Ph.D. in chemical engineering, I went off to universities in New York City and Vienna, Austria, for postdoctoral fellowships. Then I moved back to New York, which I really liked.

In fact, liking New York so much was part of why I decided to quit engineering—there weren't enough chemical engineering projects in the area. Anyway, I also wanted a more fast-paced and glamorous career.

In the meantime I started doing volunteer work for an organization known as New York Cares, which lets people do volunteer work on any schedule—projects are available in the early morning, evenings, and especially on weekends. The group has a core staff of twenty-five people and organizes from eighty to one hundred projects a month, each lasting about four hours. These projects are described in a monthly brochure, and if a volunteer wants more information, he calls a team leader. I liked the work so much that eventually I became one of those leaders.

Through the organization I was working at the One City Café, a not-for-profit restaurant training the homeless to be chefs or staff. The rest of us would help out clearing tables, slicing bread, things like that. There I met a woman who worked in the risk-management division of a major financial institution. I told her that I wanted to get out of chemical engineering; she told me she also had a technical background—mechanical engineering—and that my résumé could actually help me get a job in risk management, too.

I was intrigued and wanted to know more, so she started coaching me on financial services, how to focus on what I wanted, how to narrow my résumé, and she loaned me a couple of financial books to show me the kinds of things she could see me doing with my background. It worked. Now that I was focused, I started looking around for a new job—and within weeks, I had one. I'm now a financial consultant at The Mutual Group, doing exactly what I wanted to do.

Now let's talk about some of the specific ways volunteerism can help *you*.

But first, I have to make one thing absolutely clear: Don't volunteer simply because you think you'll reap personal rewards. You cannot be an effective volunteer if you're thinking only about yourself. Volunteerism only works when your heart, your soul, and your mind are all deeply committed. Then, and only then, can any of volunteerism's positive effects come into play.

And what are these effects? They are varied and numerous. Below you'll find a list of eleven. There are probably many more—this is only a start. If you know of other ways that volunteerism has impacted your or a friend's life, please write and let me know, so that I can add to what I hope will be a constantly developing inventory.

*1. Being a volunteer expands, complements, and enhances your professional résumé. Prospective bosses not only notice this kind of service, but it influences their hiring decisions. And when you help others, you help yourself, because you build character, and character is one of the keys to a successful career.*

While working as CEO at Ward Howell, I looked over some 150 résumés a week, even after my staff had rigorously screened the many more that came in. I don't care what anyone else says: Résumés are extremely important, for they serve as your primary introduction, and they can lead you to that crucial interview.

Besides examining the usual credentials, such as education and background, I always looked to see what sort of community and volunteer activities the applicant listed on the résumé. To me, evidence of such work was highly important; what it meant was that the person wasn't one-dimensional, that he or she wasn't absorbed only in chasing a buck—in other words, that the applicant had a solid character.

Character is very difficult to analyze. References aren't always valuable. People often won't tell you the real story behind an applicant.

For instance, one Chicago-area CEO I know wanted to fill a slot for a vice president's job and had interviewed fifteen people before running into a young man from the West Coast who brought with him a slew of recommendations, all testifying to his outstanding abilities. My friend liked the young man, but he noticed a complete absence of anything in his past indicating interests outside the office—no volunteer work, no community activity. And that led him to go back and read the recommendations more carefully. Now he was struck by what they didn't say, rather than what they did. All of them talked about his intelligence and his drive. Not a one said a word about liking him, or about enjoying working with him.

And when my friend did a little more investigation, he found that no one had lied on those recommendations. The applicant was indeed smart. But it turned out he was also impossibly ambitious, to the degree that he was threatening the stability of his entire office. None of his superiors was willing to lie for him, but they were all so hopeful he'd leave they were happy to write recommendations ignoring his fatal flaw.

I certainly wasn't the only recruitment executive looking for volunteer experience. It is a standard criterion in the field; its importance is something an inexplicable number of job applicants fail to understand.

Gerald Roach, often referred to as the "Dean of Executive Search" and currently the chairman of Heidrick and Struggles, the world's second-largest executive search firm, makes time to serve on five not-for-profit boards of directors. Roach has placed scores of Fortune 500 CEOs, including Lou Gerstner at IBM and George Fisher at Kodak. He says, "I always look for volunteer work in a candidate's background as evidence of core character attributes and the values essential to any senior executive's success. And I think everyone else in my field who's successful does, too."

Here's what John Whitehead, former co-CEO of the investment banking concern Goldman Sachs, and currently chairman of AEA Investors, a major venture-capital firm, says about his volunteer work throughout his career:

"Not only was my volunteer work from college very important in my being hired at Goldman Sachs; when I was in a position to do hiring myself, I always looked at extracurricular activities as being an indication of a variety of things. Not-for-profit activities also aided my progress up the ladder at Goldman Sachs, where the most active and most knowledgeable person was traditionally most likely to become senior partner. Certainly we found that one way to achieve that status was through not-for-profit work."

And finally, there is Paul Ray, the chairman and CEO of Ray and Berndtson, another one of the largest executive-search firms in the world. Paul himself has been very involved in community service all his life, and was recently honored with a special award by the Association of Executive Search Consultants for excellence in community service, as well as in his field. It's called the Ellie Raynolds Award, which I am pleased to say is named after my late wife. Ray says:

"There is no question that the most important part of an applicant's résumé is his or her professional experience. But there's also no question that I always look for volunteer experience. It means something important: that the individual has an involvement in the community. And that, in turn, suggests someone whose base is broader than their work alone. Someone who's not one-dimensional.

"By the way, it doesn't always speak to character, since there are some people whose motivation to volunteer is that it looks good on their résumé. So frankly, I'm more interested in what they did, and how they talk about it, rather than the mere fact that they did it."

Personally, I don't think any boss ever underestimates the importance of values when hiring a new staff member. Wayne Calloway, who recently stepped down as CEO of PepsiCo after a long and successful tenure, has said that there are six primary reasons why people fail at a job. None of them involves a lack of intelligence, or an inferior education, or the wrong experience. People fail because of character. That's right: character.

Calloway's six reasons are:

- Arrogance, which kills teamwork.
- Playing politics, which can eviscerate any company.
- Lack of perseverance, signifying the inability to follow through on a job.

- The inability to handle pressure, which is a killer, since none of us has ever heard of a job in the business world that wasn't accompanied by pressure.
- Inflexibility. This is a fatal flaw, for the world changes too fast for anyone, no matter how otherwise qualified and smart, not to remain mentally and emotionally agile at work.
- Lack of loyalty. Loyalty may be the workplace's most underrated quality, because without it, no business organization can truly thrive.

Here's my bottom line on character: a great place to develop it is in the volunteer world.

*2. When you participate in volunteer activities, you can make new and important contacts. It isn't always easy to meet people who can further your professional life and offer you advancement. But volunteerism opens the door to connections you might not ever have imagined.*

This concept couldn't be simpler. When you venture out in the world beyond your workplace, when you travel past familiar settings into the larger universe, you can't help but meet people. And some of these new friends can be the best thing that ever happened to your career.

Expanding your range of contacts offers any number of benefits. Some of them are obvious. If you're in a position in which you're required to bring in outside business, it's an excellent way to meet like-minded people you might otherwise never connect with. If you're in an area in which job security is minimal, how better to feel secure than to know important people in your field at other companies? If you work at a firm where prestige is important, what easier way to meet people whom you might otherwise read about only in the newspapers?

I can tell you of numerous good men and women who have made beneficial contacts while working hard for a volunteer cause. A brief example: Roxanne Paulson, in her mid 30s, has been working at Estee Lauder for more than ten years. Originally her job was in the Aramis division, where her department was being downsized; normally this would have meant that she was out of a job. But Roxanne's volunteer work saved her. For years she had been working with New York Cares, the same organization for which Jeffrey Smart volunteered.

Because of this work, and because of some of the contacts Roxanne had made doing it, her supervisor told her point blank that the company didn't want to lose her, and she was transferred to another division.

"I would have been out of a job," she says, "if it hadn't been for my work at New York Cares. My employers were not only impressed with what it said for my character, but frankly, by the fact that it meant I could call up senior executives of companies I had met through it."

Says John Whitehead, "Active involvement in not-for-profit organizations changes your image in the eyes of people in the outside world, many of whom are customers and clients. And serving on the board of an important organization was not only good for the organization—I hope—but also good for me as an individual. Because it gave me contacts with other important people in a situation where I wasn't soliciting business for Goldman Sachs. It put me on a different basis with people than would otherwise have been the case."

Whenever I've wanted to make a change in my career, which, as noted, has been often, almost always I was saved by the people I've met through my good works. And many times I've helped these same people in their careers.

## JUDY MILESTONE'S STORY

Back in the early 1980s I was the president of the Atlanta Smith Club, where we were doing the usual college club activities: fundraising, recruiting, trying to help out students. My husband and I had moved to Georgia from Connecticut about three years earlier, and I was jobless, staying home with our five-year-old son.

One winter afternoon in 1981, the club members were sitting around discussing Smith College–related issues when one of my colleagues mentioned that someone named Ted Turner was starting an international news network, and that she was going to do some freelance work for him, since the headquarters were in Atlanta.

"Why would he want to do such a thing in Atlanta?" I asked in my typically Northeastern way. The woman took umbrage, and so even though she didn't know me well, she said, "Why don't you come see it for yourself?"

"Sure," I said. I'd never been to a TV station and I figured it would be a nice way to kill a few hours. So the next day I went over to this basement in an old country club which had been turned into a studio. It was such a friendly operation that even though they didn't have a clue as to who I was, they walked me around the studio, and told me all about satellite interviews, which I'd never heard of.

What impressed me was that they all seemed to have a genuine sense of mission, that they were going to do something new and different. Ted Turner's idea was that if he could air an English-language newscast around the world, and people started understanding each other's viewpoints, it might make it less likely for them to go to war with each other. I was really taken with that.

Out of the blue they asked if I'd like a job—they needed someone to find and interview people over the phone for a new talk show. I thought about it for fifteen seconds and said yes. I didn't even tell my husband. I started right afterward, and we did a terrific show for five years: news stories, public-policy debates, stars, sports, business.

Today I'm the vice president of network booking, which means that I'm responsible for arranging the live guest interviews on both the domestic and international feeds, as well as a service we call Guest Source, which consists of high-profile guest interviews that can be customized for local affiliates.

The bottom line is: They hired me without looking at a résumé. I never understood why, but I've always presumed it was due to the Smith connection.

## LINDA KLECKNER'S STORY

I started working in the federal government even before I graduated from law school, at the General Services Administration Board of Contract Appeals. I was also doing volunteer work for the National Organization for Women (NOW); this was at a time when Congress had passed the Equal Credit Opportunity Act (ECOA), and the regulations were in the process of being developed.

Among other things, ECOA guaranteed women and other protected groups freedom from discrimination in credit, as well as the right to have credit in their own names with a separate credit file. As a representative of NOW, I had to testify in Congress before Senator William Proxmire's Financial Services Committee.

A few years later the Federal Reserve Board was considering starting a federal Consumer Advisory Council (CAC), and they went to the Financial Services Committee and asked for the names of people who might be hired to represent various viewpoints on the CAC. The CAC's purpose was to advise the Board of Governors of the Federal Reserve on consumer-credit regulations and related policy matters.

Proxmire's people remembered, and recommended, me. So as result of my NOW work and my testifying before Congress, I was recommended to be on the Consumer Advisory Counsel to the Federal Reserve. Now, this wasn't a real job, either—it met four times a year to advise the Federal Reserve on consumer-credit issues. But it was quite an honor, since I was a relatively low-level government employee, and many of the others on the board were college presidents and CEOs of major corporations.

Not long afterward a new person was appointed head of the National Credit Union Administration, a small government agency that regulates credit unions. Since this man used to work at the Fed, he went to people there and said he wanted to start a consumer compliance examination program, and needed someone to run it. So, because I had been on the CAC, I got the job. For someone like me who's genuinely interested in these sorts of things, it was a perfect position.

The job was particularly fulfilling, because many years earlier I myself had been denied credit. My husband and I applied for a mortgage a couple of months before I graduated from law school, and even though I was already working full time, they told me that they couldn't count my income toward the mortgage because I was "ripe"—in other words, I was statistically likely to have two children. I thought this was highly discriminatory against women, but there was nothing I could do about it. Of course I wanted to work. Why else would I have gone to law school? But they'd only consider my husband's income when making their decision.

It was because I found this so unfair that I had become interested in the whole topic of credit. So it was a real thrill: There I was with a hand in writing the regulations that the Fed put into effect, which stated that lenders couldn't use statistical calculations to exclude a woman's income. I think it was a kind of poetic justice.

*3. One of the primary issues in building a career is the need to increase your profile. But so many people tell me that the kind of relentless self-promotion they see in some of their peers is out of the question. So volunteering can be a way to let others inside and outside your industry know who you are without showboating.*

In this media-driven world, sometimes it seems that the only way to make a name for yourself is to marry a celebrity or hire a press agent. How else can you raise your profile, since doing a job quietly and efficiently seems to get you nowhere?

I'd like to think that most people don't participate in overblown self-aggrandizement. They don't relish the thought of talking only about themselves, thinking only about themselves, and acting only for themselves.

Nonetheless, letting others know about you and your work can help your career.

Good works are one of the best means of getting your name out in the professional community without feeling shameless.

For instance, after I graduated from college, I moved to Salinas, California, where I was selling a strange foreign car that few Americans had ever seen—the Volkswagen. My mentor at the time was a distant relative named Carl Voss, who told me in no uncertain terms that, in order for my business to be accepted in town, it was essential that I be accepted, too. To attain that, Carl recommended I become involved in the community, and so he introduced me to the Red Cross, the Junior Chamber of Commerce, and numerous other local organizations.

Carl's advice proved correct. Not only did these groups provide me with the chance to do some solid, valuable work in the community, they helped me become known as a person of integrity. Eventually I took on leadership roles in these organizations, and since I was only in my late twenties at the time, all of it was a learning experience for me.

This advice doesn't apply, by the way, if your only intention is to use the organization to further your career. People aren't stupid. Intentions are difficult to hide. If you are present at the organization only on the days the photographers are there, no one's going to miss the coincidence, and in the long run you'll do damage to your reputation, for you'll be known as the person who tried to take advantage of volunteerism. And that defeats the very purpose that brought you there.

A friend was recently telling me about a vice president at a large company that sponsored a cancer walk-a-thon. The vice president proclaimed his fervent devotion to this event, fully aware that the company's president considered it to be his own cause also. The vice president did everything he could to let people know how arduous the walk was, but how very important it was that everyone participate.

Then came the day of the event. The vice president made a big deal of the strenuous effort he'd put into it, although no one else in the company recalled actually seeing him during the walk. Still, he was basking in his glory—until his assistant, horrified, let the truth be known: The only time her boss could be seen walking anywhere at all were those moments when the cameras were focused on him. This news spread around the office a lot faster than the vice president's actual taxicab ride to the finish line.

Anyone working at a high level in an organization has had experience dealing with dishonest people who try to use their volunteer work for their own purposes. Once, at Outward Bound, I remember getting a phone call from a man who claimed that we stood for everything he admired and that he was interested in becoming involved as a board member. He indicated that he had very deep pockets and was a major philanthropist. Unfortunately, a short time later, the caller—Ivan Boesky—was indicted and eventually went to prison for insider trading.

Among the people I've known through Outward Bound whose visibility has increased through the honest hard work he's done is Bill Phillips, former CEO of the advertising giant Ogilvy and Mather. Bill served as chairman of International Outward Bound until last year, and was also one of the founders of The New York City Outward Bound Center, which helps thousands of inner-city kids each year.

Not only did Bill enjoy his Outward Bound work immensely, he found that his participation helped him with his international clients, thanks to Outward Bound's international scope and its blue-ribbon board of directors from around the world. He also feels that his close association with Outward Bound and its values system was admired by other senior executives.

Still another Outward Bound volunteer comes to mind: Neil Fox, formerly head of marketing for Vermont Castings Iron Stoves, was a board member who went on to start his own advertising agency, Fox MM Direct. He believes that without the contacts he made at Outward Bound, his new business wouldn't have gotten off to such a good start.

Here's what Marshall Loeb, former managing editor of *Fortune* magazine and currently a professor at Columbia University's School of Journalism, has to say: "One of my activities is serving on the Board of Trustees of the Stern School of Business of New York University. There I've encountered a marvelous cross-section of some of the best thinkers in the region.

I've also interviewed leading chief executive officers from corporate America before audiences of students, faculty, and other business leaders from the New York area. Not only has this helped keep me visible, it's continued to exercise and sharpen whatever journalistic skills I may have."

As you can see, it's possible to let other people know who you are without a staff of publicists. Through volunteer work, you can do it in a way that not only helps you, but benefits the organization to which you've donated your time and sweat.

## D.J. JAFFE'S STORY

The other day I was reading Benjamin Franklin's memoirs, in which he described how his volunteer work, like creating a fire department and a lending library, had helped him meet a lot of government officials. As a result of those contacts, he landed the general contract for the Pennsylvania Assembly's printing—that's how his print shop beat out a better-established competitor.

It's worked well for me, too, although maybe not quite as well as it did for Franklin. I consider myself to hold two positions. One is at work, where I'm a paid creative director at an advertising company. The other is at the National Alliance of the Mentally Ill (NAMI), where I'm on the board of directors. NAMI's a terrific organization, and it does outstanding work.

It's also had some unexpected effects on my career, particularly in terms of my industry profile, which is much greater than it otherwise would be. Twice *Adweek* has written about me in composite articles about people who do volunteer work outside of their jobs in advertising. And it's increased my visibility within my own company, as other senior executives have often come to me for advice when someone in their family developed a brain disorder.

Actually, I've been both awed and gratified by how supportive my company has been with what I do. I was worried that they'd disapprove of my efforts because of the sensitivity of the issue and the amount of time I dedicate to it. But the opposite's been true. They've even made donations to the cause, which has turned me into a more loyal employee, since I'd hardly want to seek a job at another company when this one's been so terrific.

The company doesn't have to do it. With outside clients, they may feel compelled to give when asked, but I'm only an employee. Their donation really means a lot, because it's not being done for self-interest. It's being done because they genuinely want to help.

The other major advantage to my volunteer work with NAMI is that I've been able to develop skills besides advertising. If for some unexpected reason I get downsized, I could get a job as a reporter on mental health issues for a trade newsletter, or as executive director of a mental health organization. I could go into not-for-profit work myself. In other words, as a result of my pro bono work, I've developed skills that have opened other career paths for me.

*4. Volunteering is an opportunity to try something new—and learn any number of new skills necessary to succeed in business. By taking a risk, you may discover aptitudes you might not otherwise learn you possess.*

I've always preached that taking a risk is one of the most important aspects of a successful business career, and I know I'm not alone. Let me tell you another story.

In the late 1950s, Joe Wilson, the founder of The Haloid Corporation, hired Ward Howell to find him a vice president of marketing. One of the candidates was a young lawyer named Peter McCullough, to whom Wilson explained his philosophy of business, which included the need for corporations to act as humane citizens in their communities. He then offered McCullough the job, but told him the pay was only $19,000 a year, which represented a 33 percent pay cut for McCullough. But McCullough decided that Wilson was too interesting a person, and Haloid too promising a company, not to take the risk. He accepted the position. Twenty-five years later, when McCullough stepped down after fifteen years as CEO, Haloid had become Xerox, which in turn had become a $15 billion company.

Nearly all the great business executives I've met have taken a similar risk at some point in their careers. Still, many people are afraid of risk, for good reason: Risks are scary.

If you're afraid to learn about risks on the job, learn about them in your volunteer work. And learn about other steps necessary to promote your career.

One of the biggest risks I ever took was simply to make a speech. For some people that may mean nothing, but I always found the idea of standing up before a group of strangers and talking at length absolutely frightening; I usually took precautions to avoid speechmaking, even if it meant jeopardizing my career. I was that afraid.

Then I went on an Outward Bound "solo," which means leaving an expedition to venture into the woods completely alone, without food or shelter, for anywhere from twelve hours to a couple of days. During a solo we encourage people to write, and I composed six haiku poems, since poetry is something I enjoy very much.

The next morning we all gathered to discuss our experiences, and I knew that despite my fear, I ought to read the poems aloud. Knees shaking, stomach clenching, and voice quivering, I did. The reception was good enough to soothe my fears about public speaking in general. I then took advantage of several volunteer opportunities to give speeches or readings, and slowly I learned that, despite my great fears, nothing bad ever happened when I talked at length to an audience. In fact, occasionally people seemed to enjoy it.

Another thing you can discover while taking risks is failure. When working at a not-for-profit, you can try out new ideas, interesting ways of managing, or unusual methods for interacting with people. If you're going to make mistakes—and everyone does—making them without putting your career on the line is probably your best bet in the long run.

You might also learn another lesson that took me years to understand: Failure can be an outstanding teacher. You may think you have hidden talents for writing, or speaking, or managing, but you never know until you try them out. When you do, you learn just a little more about yourself and your abilities.

I have a friend in public relations who dreamed of becoming a professional artist, but all he ever did was doodle and sketch. Then he took a position at a service organization, where he volunteered to create a line of posters. He discovered, to his dismay, that he wasn't very talented. His daydreams crashed to earth. But once he recovered, he was able to get back to what he did do extremely well, without spending half the day wishing he was doing something else.

## CATHERINE MOBLEY'S STORY

I've done all kinds of volunteer work throughout my life, at the Clemson City Council, the Sierra Club, the Columbia Light House for the Blind, a rape crisis line, a domestic violence program, and so on. My full time job, however, is teaching sociology at Clemson University.

Volunteerism has helped me in many ways: It's let me experiment with different skills that I was either afraid to use on the job, or had had no opportunity to try out.

For instance, I've learned presentation skills. At the domestic-violence program my superiors asked me to put together a fifteen-minute seminar on discipline—the best way for parents to give it, and how kids usually react to it. The families I helped were required to go through this program, but that didn't necessarily mean that they were interested in what I had to say—in fact, in many cases, they weren't at all. So I had to learn how to organize a presentation for an audience who attended because they had to, not because they wanted to. This experience proved invaluable in my career choice—teaching. I'm basically on stage every day now, and I owe some of my success as a teacher to learning how to speak at the violence program.

Most of all, volunteer experience has allowed me to gain insight into a variety of career options. For example, some years ago I considered going back to school to get my Ph.D. in social work. But first I decided to see how it felt to do some hands-on work, so I helped out with the parent-nurturing program in a domestic violence program, designed for parents referred by the courts. I figured this would give me some excellent exposure to family casework, since both parents and their children participated.

I volunteered every other week for a year, and it was soon clear that I didn't want a Ph.D. after all. I loved the work, but when I tried to envision doing it all the time, I couldn't; I thought I'd burn out working so closely with families who were continually troubled. And because I realized I also wanted to do research and teach, the social work route wasn't right for me. Fortunately I discovered this before going off to graduate school.

## TOM BROWN'S STORY

I started doing volunteer work when I was really young, and intended to keep doing it when I went to the University of Texas, San Antonio (UTSA). What I most wanted to do was join Alpha Phi Omega, the national coed service fraternity, but UTSA didn't have a chapter; when the national office asked me if I'd like to start one, I agreed. The UTSA student activities office noticed my work and asked if I wanted to attend a national COOL conference. COOL is the Campus Outreach Opportunity League, a national not-for-profit organization founded in 1984 that helps college students expand their community-service programs. Soon after that, we started a branch of COOL at UTSA. That in turn led to my working with Christmas in April USA, which rebuilds homes for low-income and disabled people so they don't have to move.

After graduation I began working at a pizza shop, but I really wanted to learn about the Internet and html coding. My employers wouldn't let me, I couldn't figure out how to get any experience, and there were no jobs available that I knew of. So I decided to volunteer to create a Web page for Christmas in April. I told them I'd have a Web page up for them in four months. They didn't know I didn't know what I was doing, but I decided to risk it, since this would force me to learn.

Now, my reputation was on the line. I went out and bought a beginner's book on Web pages, read it all, and then just followed the directions. So there I was, with a new skill.

All this led to my next job. I was working part time at UTSA, where they were interested in putting together a departmental Web page. Since I'd been bragging about what I'd been able to do for Christmas in April, suddenly I was creating one for them, too. And when a UTSA alumna called, looking to hire someone to put together a Web page for her business, UTSA recommended me. As far as I'm concerned, it's the perfect position. I got my wish—I'm now a Web page pro.

*5. Even great jobs can be boring now and then. Volunteering will supply your mind with something new and invigorating. And that can lead you to fresh, surprising places.*

How many times in my career have people asked me for guidance because they'd lost interest in their current job? More often than I'd like to count. These were generally good people with good jobs, good salaries, and good prospects who were nonetheless unhappy. The job wasn't fulfilling, their coworkers weren't exciting, the work was deadening.

"I don't care about my work as much I used to," these job-seekers would say. Or, "I feel as though my mind has stalled and I'm not learning anything anymore." Boredom, frustration, and restlessness seemed to be all they could feel.

The truth is that few people enjoy an idle mind, whereas a challenging position can be one of life's greatest motivators. But jobs aren't always like that, and you can't quit every time things get dull.

Here's what good works can do to alleviate this situation: They can enable you to work at something that takes a talent you've never used on the job and exercise a part of your mind that's otherwise idle.

For instance, I know an excellent CPA who, although terrifically skilled with numbers, always wanted to write. He knew he could never abandon work to start a career as a starving author; he had to support his wife and kids. So he volunteered to work with a drug-rehabilitation center, where he was eventually called upon to write their annual report. It wasn't the Great American Novel, but nonetheless the task gave the man a chance to create something that made him happy, without jeopardizing his current job. The result was an improvement in his work at his regular job, along with a better relationship with his boss, who had become exasperated by his relentless complaining.

Too often in our lives we become stuck: Our jobs seem repetitive, and we don't see the upward trajectory of progress. We feel we've stopped learning. But by stepping outside the daily grind into a different environment, we can again feel a sense of progress, which helps us get unstuck.

I know many people who, bored or dissatisfied with their own jobs, turned to volunteer work for relief, and found that without realizing it, they had discovered a new career. Here are two instances:

## MITCH CRANE'S STORY

For me, it all started while I was chairing Ted Kennedy's 1980 presidential campaign in southeast Pennsylvania, where I became friendly with a young man heading up the Kennedy contingent at West Chester University. He'd worked very hard for me, and we stayed in touch.

The next fall my friend approached me and said he'd been elected president of a new campus fraternity, Sigma Phi Epsilon, and they were looking for someone in the community to help them buy a house. I said I wasn't interested, because I wasn't pro-fraternity. In fact, I'd been very anti-fraternity during my own college years, and no amount of begging and pleading was going to change that. At heart I was still a 1960s kind of guy.

"But you owe me a favor," he insisted—and it was true. So I went to the fraternity to meet the guys, who turned out to be responsible, decent people—so much so that I changed my mind, agreed to help, and within three months they had their house.

Later that year I was running for a position as a municipal judge, and in return for my help, the guys campaigned for me, registering students to vote, canvassing the neighborhoods. In Pennsylvania many judicial offices allow cross-filing, and candidates can run on each party's ballot—the idea being to try to make the judicial selection less political. So I was on both ballots. The Republican Party endorsed the incumbent I was running against, but with the help of my new campaign staff, not only did I win the Democratic primary, I also won the Republican primary—by two votes.

Not surprisingly, my relationship with the fraternity warmed, so much so that a few months after my election I was initiated into Sigma Phi Epsilon. I never thought I'd ever go Greek, but I was too impressed by the place to say no.

I'm not saying fraternity life is perfect, but this particular fraternity interested me because, earlier than most, they'd adopted strong anti-alcohol policies, banned kegs and hazing, and they were having real discussions about sexism and homophobia. I was impressed.

Meanwhile, now that I was a public figure on the bench and had a strong, positive view of fraternities, I began to get invitations to speak, such as at a hazing panel discussion at the NorthEastern Inter-Fraternity Conference, in New Brunswick, New Jersey. Hazing had never interested me before, but I did a good deal of research and discovered that I had something to say: I was strongly against it, since it was hard to reconcile the good things I saw in a fraternity as decent as West Chester's Sigma Phi Epsilon with something as stupid as hazing.

Voluntary public speaking turned out to be enormously enjoyable, and I decided to put together a program. Soon I was talking on campuses around the East Coast, usually about such risk-management issues as drugs, alcohol, and hazing.

One day someone handed me a check. It hadn't really occurred to me that I could be paid for this—I enjoyed it too much to think about money.

Meanwhile, I was getting bored with my job, so after six years I stepped down from the judgeship and returned to my law practice. Soon I found that too mundane to be of much interest, either. So I thought more about public speaking and decided that it might be a good way to supplement my income and do something I thought was important.

By June 1997 I had given speeches at more than 130 campuses coast to coast, mostly about risk management: how fraternities can properly protect their facility, how to handle lawsuits and criminal actions. I tell my audiences that one of the best ways to do this is to lead a life in harmony with the stated values of the fraternity. What's our purpose here? I ask. Are we trying to train young men to be successful citizens, or are we fooling ourselves?

Speaking is now a half-time job, and I'm on my way to making it full time. This gives me more satisfaction on a regular basis than anything else I've ever done. For one thing, I can see the effect I have on people. I recently talked about date rape, and later received a letter from a woman saying, "I thought you were talking about me, because this happened to me as a freshman. I never told anyone before, and now I want to do something about it." And once, after talking about drunk driving, I got a letter from a young man who told me that my speech made him throw his false drivers' license into a sewer. That means a lot to me. What's more important than touching someone else's life and making it better?

## KIM REED'S STORY

Everyone always assumed that I was going to be a lawyer. I'd done well in school, I was a good writer, and I had strongly held beliefs. So, without much more thought, I went off to the University of Virginia Law School.

At the time, I loved it, and I did all the things I was supposed to do: worked on the law journal, served as class president, and so on. When I graduated, again I just went with the flow, interviewing with all the large law firms. Because I'd done well at moot court—which is essentially a courtroom arguing competition—I told the firms I wanted to be a litigator. Now, I didn't know what a litigator at a big firm really did. I just thought it was like being Perry Mason.

So, in 1989 I accepted a job at a major Los Angeles law firm with a starting salary of $75,000, plus bonus. They put me right to work on big cases: antitrust, white-collar crime, insurance defense, and entertainment litigation. I had a good time: It was all new and sexy, I was meeting smart people, my firm was prestigious.

But after a year I'd become dissatisfied. The cases were no longer interesting, and the work wasn't meaningful. Meanwhile, I'd become engaged to someone on the East Coast, and in mid-1992 I moved to D.C. Because I still owed more than $35,000 in student loans, I didn't consider changing careers, and landed a job at a huge, high-powered firm, doing commercial litigation for Fortune 100 corporations. But I liked the fact that the firm encouraged pro bono work, and I immediately volunteered for the Whitman Walker AIDS Clinic, Washington Lawyers for Civil Rights, and the Coalition to Stop Gun Violence, among other causes.

I loved this work far more than my day job, where, soon enough, I was miserable, walking into the office every morning, shutting my door, and crying. And I couldn't talk about it, because it's career suicide at a big law firm to let anyone think you're less than 100 percent invested in your job.

The event that really put me over the edge was my 1994 annual review, after I'd completed a grueling year, working fourteen hours a day, seven days a week, even sleeping on a futon in my office several nights a week. During this review they told me that my work was excellent and I was on partnership track, but that I didn't seem to be committed to the firm. When pressed, they said I cared more about my outside activities than my job. In other words, I felt I was being told to choose between my work at the firm and my volunteer work. Only then did I realize how much all of those outside activities meant to me, and how much I was just going through the motions at the firm.

In desperation, I confided in a friend, who told me that she was seeing a career counselor, whom I now started seeing, too. Soon I discovered I couldn't stand my job for several reasons: I hate conflict, I hate fighting; I love helping individuals and seeing the results of my work on an individual basis; and I need a lot of positive feedback and appreciation.

But I still had big student-loan payments, so I couldn't go off and do something like work for Legal Services full time.

Then a friend got a call from the Dean of the University of North Carolina Law School, asking if she knew anyone who might be interested in becoming dean of career development and placement at UNC Law School. Well, among the other volunteer work I'd been doing was career counseling for lawyers—I'd been chairing the career development section of the D.C. Bar Association. And at the AIDS clinic, I'd been tutoring and working with kids; furthermore, serving on an advisory board on mental health in the D.C. schools had helped me develop some strong counseling abilities.

I sent in my résumé, a week later I was interviewing, and three weeks after that I had the job. My boss later told me I got the job over all the other lawyers who applied because my volunteer work convinced them I could handle the position.

So now I'm being paid to help people. The feedback I get from the students proves to me that I'm making a difference. They feel I'm here to assist them, that I'm their friend during a stressful period in their lives. And I *still* work seventy or eighty hours a week—but now I do it because I want to, not because I have to.

6. *Growing a career can be difficult. Few people show up at a job with their talents full blown. You need to learn so much, and yet learning experiences can be hard to come by. But you can pick up these skills by volunteering.*

When taking management-training courses or business-school classes, you're often presented with problem-solving assignments—situations that teach you how to manage, how to work with others, and so on. Working at a not-for-profit can teach you some of these same lessons. Each organization is different, and you won't know ahead of time what you might learn, but nonetheless it's highly likely that the kinds of issues you'll run into won't be very different from those you struggle with on the job.

Anyone who takes a leadership role at a not-for-profit must deal with leading a disparate group of people in various situations. You'll quickly learn how to be a team player, because your peers are there only because they want to be, not because they have to be. If you're a leader, and the environment you create isn't motivating and positive, they won't be volunteers much longer—not for you, at least.

Furthermore, when you're responsible for decision-making, such as serving as a committee chair or as an office or project director, if you can't involve the others on your committee, you may well lose their confidence, and perhaps their participation.

Here's an obvious example. Recently a foundation I know launched a search for a chief operating officer. The board member heading up the search committee operated not unlike the old kremlin: He kept information shrouded in secrecy, refused to discuss his actions with other members of the search committee, and finally offered the job to someone no one else had met.

Luckily, the woman turned down the job; if she had taken it under those auspices, she would have had a very difficult time.

The upshot of this story is that the foundation is now in chaos, trying to cope with the unpleasant residue left behind by the board member's search process. On top of that, they still haven't hired their number-two person.

In my own life, my work as a young man in Salinas offered me many chances to pick up numerous new business skills, since it exposed me to the politics of organizations other than car dealerships, which was all I knew at the time.

When I became president of the local chapter of the Red Cross, one of the first things the board instructed me to do was to fire a key member of my staff. Although the woman had been on the job for many years, her work was poor, and everyone wanted her gone—but they'd waited for me to do the job. So I dutifully knocked on her door and told her that she was no longer needed. Upset and angry, she blamed me for her ouster. This was a tough life experience; I'd never fired anyone before, and it was something I had to learn how to do.

Besides picking up firing experience, I also learned hiring skills. When I first showed up at Outward Bound's national office, it had a poor reputation within the entire Outward Bound system due to its lack of experienced professionals in key positions such as marketing, finance, and fund-raising. All in all, I had to replace a dozen people my first year.

Here's what Frances Hesselbein, former head of the Girl Scouts of the

USA and currently CEO of the Drucker Foundation, a not-for-profit dedicated to improving management techniques in not-for-profit organizations, has to say:

"When I work with graduate students in business schools, they say, 'In the mid-seventies there weren't very many women in business schools. So where did you get your early business training?' I tell them that my first real management training came from working with Girl Scout Troop 17, where I learned the team approach to management, also known as the Patrol System.

"They crack up. But it's true that if we take our work as volunteers seriously, we can learn the basic principles of management and leadership. And indeed they are basic, they are generic, and they are fundamental, and they carry right across the three sectors.

"Volunteer work gives you an unlimited opportunity to create your individual approach to management and leadership and development of materials. It's amazing to me how the volunteers in this country, in community after community, are exemplifying some of the best practices that the businesses talk about.

"And it's not just learning management and leadership skills. It's also the freedom to develop new approaches. I found unlimited freedom and opportunity to throw out the old hierarchy and really build a flexible and fluid management system that was part of the future, not just re-treading or re-plowing the old furrows."

Says Arthur Sulzberger, Jr., publisher of *The New York Times*: "One of the great values of a not-for-profit is that you deal with people who don't have to be there. They can walk away at any time that they find you've become a pain. And that means that your leadership style has to be a collective one—in other words, you learn how to make a group of people comfortable with you, and their task."

These are important skills to learn, because the old days of command and control in the private sector, where decisions were made from the top, are gone. They're gone because there are more options than ever before for workers, who now have the freedom to take their many profitable skills to other jobs. This means that, as a boss, you've got to keep your employees motivated, and pleased to be part of your organization.

And that's something you can learn at not-for-profits.

## AUBREY HAWES' STORY

I first came to New York from a small Massachusetts fishing village in 1966. I wanted to work in advertising, and I spent fifteen years doing just that. Then one day I was pitching Chase Manhattan Bank for my agency; we won the business, but then Chase asked me to come work for them. I thought a two-year stay there would look great on my résumé, but I'm still here sixteen years later. Today I'm Chase's corporate director of marketing resources, which includes responsibility for advertising, creative services, cultural sponsorships, sports marketing, the Chase art collection, the Chase archives, market research, and the Internet.

Probably one of my most visible acts as a volunteer happened when I was working with WNET, New York's Channel 13, the Public Broadcasting station. Chase always sends a group of volunteers to pitch in on fund-raising nights. The first time I went along I noticed the phones weren't ringing. So I announced that Chase would put up a matching grant, but no one understood what I meant. I continued: If someone calls and promises to donate, say, $100, Chase will match that pledge. No one had offered to do this before, but it worked wonderfully, and the station developed a formal grant-matching program.

I've volunteered at many other places over the years, such as at a child-care agency which was once in serious financial jeopardy. With two other board members I offered to look at the budget and try to get it back on course; it was soon clear that the agency was eating up its endowment and had only about three years left to survive. They simply weren't generating enough income to offset their operating expenses.

This situation gave me an opportunity to use some of my marketing skills and apply them to a not-for-profit. And in the process I learned how to look at profit-and-loss statements for the first time, I learned how to work with a board of directors, and I gained experience in stabilizing an organization. In other words, the situation, dire as it was, helped me develop a whole new set of business skills.

Included in those skills was the ability to communicate: I had to convince the board of directors to take a 180-degree turn in their vision, as well as to manage our suggested cuts so as not to disrupt the staff. We eventually explained how to eliminate the deficit through expense-cutting and instituting a stronger development office. The board voted unanimously in favor of our proposal, and the agency got back on its feet.

One final note. When you're working with other volunteers, you have to motivate people to perform without making money as a goal. You can always get people to come to a meeting and raise their hand to volunteer, but if you don't tell them what to do, 90 percent of them aren't going to do anything at all. You have to devise ways to work with people that a salaried job may never teach you.

## TOD HAMACHEK'S STORY

After leaving Harvard Business School I eventually moved to my home town, Portland, Oregon, where I took a job with a company that made malt for the brewing industry. Eventually I became its CEO.

Once in Portland I became involved with the local art museum and also joined the board of a not-for-profit crafts gallery, which had two divisions, a craft gallery with rotating exhibits and a sales gallery. This position proved to be a great challenge, and I probably learned more in my four years there than I did from any other board experience.

Our issue was figuring how to market an organization, whether for profit or not. The gallery provided a business-school textbook case.

For instance, the gallery had no arrangements to ship packages, so if someone wanted to buy a wedding present, he couldn't have it sent. The gallery just told customers, "Here's a box, you go do it." Also, store hours weren't convenient for the clientele, and it never merchandized its holdings, in print or otherwise.

Fortunately, also serving with me on that board was the late Harold Hirsch, who had founded White Stag, the clothing company. Harold was a consummate retailer, and he taught me a great deal. [By the way, this is another advantage to serving on volunteer boards: exposure to senior people you wouldn't ordinarily meet.]

With Harold, the board worked through all the various problems in order to make the gallery more consumer-oriented. I'd taken a marketing class in business school, and I'd worked in industrial sales, but this was my first exposure to the retail market. I learned that consumer marketing is far more sophisticated than on the industrial side.

All my work with the gallery was directly applicable to my job at my own company, where we were struggling to distinguish ourselves from our competitors. The issue was exactly like that at the crafts gallery: how to make it easier for others to do business with us.

A few years later, I was invited to join the board of the Northwest Outward Bound School, which was going through some bad times—enrollment was dropping, revenues decreasing. So I started attending meetings, working my way up through various positions until I became vice chair of the board.

The school's basic plan was to retrench and lay people off in order to survive. I disagreed. I thought that first and foremost we were in the mail-order business, and that we needed a terrific catalog of courses to be sent out to prospective customers. I told the executive director it was a mistake to cut back, that instead we needed to grow, using the mail-order business as our base. I wanted to bring someone on the board who understood that business. So we asked John Emrick, head of Portland's highly successful Norm Thompson Company, to join us.

John agreed, and with other board members, we started putting together a strategic plan. John then created the school's first real catalog. The other schools weren't impressed; in fact, they told us we were selling out the soul of Outward Bound. But the catalog was spectacularly successful—in a year and a half we doubled our enrollment. Today it's still the basic format used to recruit participants for Outward Bound schools.

That experience was invaluable because it was my first opportunity to think through an organization's future plans on a conceptual basis. It's one reason why today, if I have one main strength, it's strategic planning. I've used the same techniques I developed at Outward Bound in various businesses I've been involved with ever since.

Another volunteer organization taught me a great deal about business. This was a place where the president had completely lost the confidence of those around him, probably the best example I've ever seen of failure of leadership. If you can't win an organization's trust, you can't motivate that organization. I also saw firsthand the value of listening: This president refused to listen to anyone. I firmly believe I wouldn't have learned this lesson so well if I hadn't seen for myself what can go wrong.

That experience led me to institute a series of roundtables at my own company, where a cross section of hourly employees met to talk about issues I never would have considered without their input. This has helped me establish a solid rapport with employees whose concerns I might not have otherwise recognized.

I don't think there's any better place to learn these lessons at a young age than at a not-for-profit. If you're bright and motivated, you can get involved at a high policy level long before you ever would in business.

By the way, I look for this kind of work when I hire senior people. It tells me several things: that they know how to manage their time, that they've had exposure to something that will help them develop other skills helpful in business, and that they'll be more empathetic and sensitive to what's going on around them.

*7. Volunteering expands your horizons. It helps you learn what others have to say in situations where you normally wouldn't venture. When you bring this wisdom back to the workplace, you'll profit from the exposure.*

Too often we become regimented by our work. We're told whom to talk to, what to think, when to think it, where to go, and why. We march to the same office every day, sit at the same desk, and meet with the same people.

But to truly advance in your career, you need exposure to other people, other places, and new ideas.

John Whitehead once told me that while running Goldman Sachs, he spent a third of his time on not-for-profit activity, because he felt he couldn't be the broad-based decision-maker Goldman needed if he received input only from inside the company.

Likewise, Reuben Mark, CEO of Colgate, and his wife Arlene "adopted" twenty-three teenagers from the South Bronx under the "I Have a Dream" program, which mentors kids and helps them prepare for college and careers; Reuben credits this opportunity with having improved his growth as a manager, making him feel more empathetic towards others, more tolerant, more understanding.

Volunteering offers you a way to learn more about yourself and to test your limits without jeopardizing your job. One young woman I know wanted to rise in her company's sales department, but she had always been afraid of opening new markets. She felt comfortable only in social arenas familiar to her, and she let others tackle areas that made her anxious. Deeply religious, this woman volunteered at an inner-city Sunday school during her spare time, working with parents and teachers as well as children. Her teaching there taught her more about the world at large than anything she'd learned in business school. Becoming comfortable with people outside her previously narrow world, she was eventually able to expand her business skills to become one of the leading salespeople in her office.

Remaining isolated inside your particular industry or work culture can destroy your ability to grow. If you don't see an opportunity to meet people with other viewpoints and other experiences, go out and lend a hand to an organization where you'll meet such people, and profit from the experience.

## ALAN MARK'S STORY

My family was very artistic, and I couldn't decide if I was going to take after them and go into music—I was once a pretty serious musician—or make my mark in the business world. After a great deal of thought, I went for the latter.

I graduated summa cum laude from the University of Pennsylvania's Wharton School with concentrations in finance and accounting and went right to Chase Manhattan in their corporate lending area, working with mining and metals companies. It was demanding work, and it mattered to me that I was successful.

In 1979 I was recruited by another company to join a new venture on the municipal finance side. A few years later, it was acquired by still a larger concern, and since I didn't want to work for such a big firm, I went off to still another place to start up a short-term finance banking business—that is, getting involved with instruments like commercial paper, demand notes, put bonds.

I did that through the 1980s, ultimately getting involved in structuring municipal swaps and other derivatives. In the early 1990s, I was asked to help start up the firm's own derivatives operations. I've been involved in this area ever since, as head of global derivatives.

My career has been terrific, and I've enjoyed it. But I was that quintessential eighties guy, working hard, moving along quickly. There was no question about it: My career was my primary focus.

Then the decade changed and so did I, and some kind of smashing feeling came over me. I'd made some money, I'd been successful, my career was going well. What did it all mean? There I was, approaching my fortieth birthday, and I was becoming reflective for the first time since I'd begun my career. Was I a good person? What was I doing? It was the strangest phenomenon. I don't know how many movies I'd seen where people ask these existential questions, but now here I was, exactly like a character in one of them.

After thinking about all this, I realized that I wanted to leave something of value behind in this world. Maybe that sounds maudlin, but I wanted to have an impact on something besides my own bank account.

I didn't have a clue where to start. And it wasn't the sort of thing I felt comfortable discussing with other people in the firm. Wall Street isn't the place for quiet introspection.

Then a good friend told me about the Big Apple Circus, where he was doing volunteer work. Circuses may not be the first thing that come to mind when thinking about helping others, but this place was different.

The Big Apple Circus is a classical circus, based on old European one-ring circus artistry, with horses, acrobatics, and juggling, but without the extra rings and exotic jungle animals. But what got me was that it was a not-for-profit heavily involved in community service, particularly the Clown Care Unit, which trains professional clowns and sends them to various hospitals to meet with terminally and chronically ill children. They work with the kids as they get wheeled down to surgery, and they deal with the families—all of this falling under the basic belief that laughter contributes to stress reduction, which in turn is critical to the kids' recovery.

I called my friend and said that I wanted to help, and eventually I became chair of the finance committee. That really gets you into the guts of an organization. If you run the money, you can learn it all.

The circus has dramatically affected my life. It's made me feel as if I'm really participating in a community outside of work, and that I'm helping the world in ways other than building up my own résumé. It's letting me understand that there's a community away from Wall Street. It means getting back to people with different economic backgrounds, people with different cares, with different immediate needs.

And it's been great for my job. It gives me a better sense of the public and it rounds out my view of the consumer market. But the most important lesson for me has been learning how to set priorities. It's a matter of perspective, something I'd been lacking. When you're watching ill children being soothed by the antics of a clown, when you're dealing with people worried about making enough money to survive, when you're facing basic issues of life and death—if you have any sense at all, you start looking at yourself differently.

As a result, I've learned that my work doesn't always have to be done at a fever pitch. I've figured out how to prioritize the critical issues, how to better manage my responsibilities. Just as life and death are more important than derivatives, so I've learned at work to decide which battles need to be fought and which can be addressed in a more accommodating way. I couldn't do that before.

All this has made me a more efficient manager, and I get along better with the people around me. It doesn't make me less driven, but it's taught me how to channel my drive, and how to make my drive more acceptable to people.

Another lesson: When you're dealing with people with different perspectives, people with whom you're not always going to get your way, you have to learn to compromise. My volunteer work has given me a new perspective on consensus building.

I've also picked up managerial skills from the circus artists. Every day I deal with traders and bankers who are as emotionally volatile as creative people, but often don't have access to their own emotional lives, so it's hard to know what's going on in their minds. The circus artists are no less volatile, but they're more transparent, more expressive. By watching them closely, I'm able to see the same kinds of emotional ups and downs my colleagues go through, and it's made me better able to understand what is going on in the minds of the people I work with in my job.

For instance, in the past I could seem dictatorial with my team. If somone had a problem, I'd say, "You go solve it." The circus taught me to sit down and say, "Let's review what the problems are here. I really understand what you're feeling, but please don't feel that way, because there's a bigger picture out there, and we'll get through it together."

In other words, I've learned how to listen to another point of view, and to help others work through difficult situations. And to defuse a lot of needless emotion that a trader might have.

I've even become more relaxed when dealing with my own superiors. I was always one of those triple type-A personalities: driven, success-oriented, a product of the '80s. Now I've been able to accept the fact that my career's going just fine. I don't have to make constant quantum leaps up the ladder. I don't always have to win. I don't have to have the last word. I'm sure my bosses appreciate that change.

*8. Sometimes the best way to land the right job is to volunteer for one. You may be amazed at how many people have found the perfect career by lending a hand.*

Not long ago I was chatting with a group of young women and men who'd come to hear me give a speech. They were all business school students, and when I asked what they wanted to do with their degrees, most had prompt replies: investment banking, mutual funds, accounting, entrepreneurial startups, teaching.

But even among a highly motivated group such as this there's always a small subgroup who, after two extra years of school, still aren't certain what they want to do for a living. And sure enough, several of these people hung behind, waiting to ask me more about my career, since I had held several jobs in various industries.

I told them not to worry. So what if you're twenty-five and you're not sure what you want to do for a living? Or if you're thirty-five, or forty-five, or older? There's no law that says everyone must find the right job by a certain age, or rot in career-placement offices for the rest of their lives. For many people, finding a position where they feel fulfilled is difficult. Yes, some people know from the age of four that they're going to be a doctor or a lawyer. But I've known plenty of others who went through an entire lifetime without being sure.

I truly believe that life is a journey, not a destination. For many of us, our first job is a step, not a terminus. We gather information from that first job, and then we may sample the workplace somewhere else, and as we do, it becomes clearer what the next step will be—and the next step may be just that, a step, and not an end. It's just not always possible to say, "I know what I'll be doing ten years from now," or "I know what I'll be doing when I grow up." Even when I was in my fifties I was asking myself, What am I going to do when I grow up?

To paraphrase Gertrude Stein, sometimes when you get there, there isn't any there there. So don't worry about getting there. It's more important that the journey itself be satisfying.

The journey can also be surprising. Sometimes what you thought was a side road turns out to be one of life's main highways. A great many people I've known have found their true calling quite unexpectedly through good works. They didn't have a clue that a volunteer position would turn into something bigger. But often doing volunteer work means participating in an organization where, even if you're working for free, not everyone else is. In fact, most volunteer organizations employ anything from a small paid staff to a large network of people. If the cause is one you support, there's no harm in considering accepting payment for your help. The money probably won't be as much as you could earn on Wall Street, but if the work is enjoyable and meaningful, then follow your heart and make a living from it.

## EDYE RUGALO'S STORY

The Young Musicians Foundation (YMF) is a forty-two-year-old not-for-profit organization that gives financial assistance and performance opportunities to gifted young musicians. We have ten other programs, including scholarships, mentorships, competitions, and concerts; we also give aspiring young conductors an opportunity to train with an orchestra before they apply for their own post. We're very proud of our alumni, which includes Michael Tilson Thomas, Andre Previn, and Lawrence Foster.

One of the reasons I first got involved in YMF is that when I was growing up I played two instruments and—I hate saying this, but it's true—my teacher told me I had real talent. But my family didn't have enough money to give me the kind of music education I needed—the private lessons, the exposure to master teachers.

I filed this experience away in some back corner of my mind, but years later, when I decided to do some volunteer work, I guess it wasn't a surprise that I found a music-oriented organization, where I started working on fundraising drives. Since my husband is in the music industry, I was able to take advantage of some of his connections to help out, and I was good at it.

I was interested in trying to build a stronger base for YMF, so I eventually created a business advisory board, because I knew that arts organization can only survive with strong ties to business. The idea was to cultivate the young middle-management person who would one day take a giant leap up the corporate ladder to become a CEO or president. And that's what happened. Many of the people we connected with years ago have landed in executive positions at places like Disney or Warner Bros., which means we now have entrée to businesses throughout the city.

From there I took a seat on YMF's board of directors for eight years, and then I was asked to take a part-time paying job with the title of general director, which was a glorified name for a fundraiser. I was no longer a volunteer.

Next, the board asked if I would consider becoming executive director for one year while they conducted a search for somone permanent for the position. After the year was up, they decided that they liked what I'd done, so they asked me to stay on full time. I agreed, and today, instead of volunteering for an organization I love, I'm being paid to run it.

Sure, years ago I wanted to perform. But instead I'm helping musicians do what I couldn't. In the long run, that's more satisfying. It makes me feel good to be involved with some of these kids, like Leila Josephowitz, who's one of the most brilliant young artists in the country today. I love the work.

A few years ago, when Miramax was making the movie *Mr. Holland's Opus,* they came in to consult with us, and some of the music featured in the picture was actually performed by our orchestra. As a result of that connection, people sometimes call me Mrs. Holland. How could anyone not like a job like this?

## ANDY CARROLL'S STORY

I'm twenty-seven, and I run APL, the American Poetry and Literacy Project, which I'd previously been doing as a volunteer for five years. It became a paying job very recently.

I'd left high school thinking I was going to be a Hollywood producer, so I went to college in Los Angeles. I've always loved the art of filmmaking, but I can't deny that I was also lured by the prospect of money, fame, power, and other enticements I'm now embarrassed to admit.

Most of all, though, I was going through a time in my life when I didn't believe in anything. We lived, we died—that was pretty much it, and I was hell-bent on getting as much out of life as possible. The sense of freedom, of being unconnected to any one faith or idea, was exhilarating. I was extremely individualistic—life for me was without restraints. It was intoxicating.

Then, in college, I took a sociology class because it was rumored to be really easy. We read a book by Robert Bellah called *Habits of the Heart,* in which he said that although Americans maintain a staunch individuality, which is good, they have to temper that with a sense of community, a sense of being a part of something greater than themselves. On top of that I read another book, *Rachel and Her Children,* by Jonathan Kozol, a day-to-day account of what it's like to be homeless in New York City. It was searing.

The one-two punch of those books had a powerful impact. I started rethinking my career, trying to get away from the self-centeredness that had been consuming me, and I ultimately transferred to school in New York City, where I became involved in several community-related activities.

I was still unsure what I wanted to do, but I was increasingly interested in the not-for-profit world and was coming to believe that there were millions of people like me who wanted to help in some way but didn't know how to make the right connection. I did some research and ended up editing a guide on making a difference called *Volunteer USA,* published in 1991. The book sold miserably, but it changed my life, for it showed me the level of commitment in America, and how many great people are out there volunteering for truly creative, resourceful not-for-profits.

Then, in 1992, a buddy handed me a transcript of a speech Joseph Brodsky had given at the Library of Congress. Brodsky won the Nobel Prize for Literature in 1987 and was the nation's poet laureate, but I'd never heard of him—which, considering that I was an English major, was kind of appalling. In the speech, Brodsky suggested that a book of poetry should be put in every hotel room in the country.

Although I wasn't a great fan of poetry at the time, literacy was an issue I strongly believed in, and I loved Brodsky's idea of getting books out to the general public. On a whim I wrote him a letter, not really expecting to hear anything back. But I'd just met some hotel executives at a dinner, and after telling them about the idea, they explained how this thing might work from their perspective. I figured Brodsky might be interested.

He was. He actually wrote back and suggested that we get together and brainstorm. It turned out he was serious about the project, and he wanted someone who had the time to write all the letters and make all the phone calls. I did, and that's how the APL Project got off the ground.

We started off by giving away a few thousand anthologies to hotels. The response was overwhelming. The hotels told us the guests were reading, enjoying, and even taking the books—which was exactly what we wanted.

Since that time the APL Project has shifted its focus a bit. Now we prefer giving the books to public schools, prisons, literacy programs, and libraries rather than putting them in hotel rooms. We also hand them out on subways, in trains, in jury waiting rooms—anyplace where we can surprise people with great words. And, we've got a huge venture with the phone book companies to publish poetry in the Yellow Pages, which means we'll have fifteen million books going out nationwide with poetry in them. Under Insurance you'll find, besides agency listings, Emily Dickinson's *I Died for Beauty* or, under Travel Agencies, Robert Frost's *The Road Not Taken*.

The original idea was that I could do this on evenings and weekends. But there's only so much you can do part time, so last winter I applied for a foundation grant to go full time—and do it. That's why I'm now being paid to do this.

A lot of my friends are just coming out of law school and business school and landing jobs with incredible salaries. I don't envy them. I make my own schedule, my job brings me into contact with amazing people, and I love the work. I've had the chance to meet a lot of other folks—some my age, some older—who began as volunteers and ultimately either started their own not-for-profit or were offered jobs with one (after making themselves indispensable). They, too, feel the same sense of passion and fulfillment, and that there's nothing in life they'd rather be doing. It's a hell of a feeling.

## DEBRA GREENWOOD'S STORY

I've been a single mother for seventeen years, and I never found a single job that made me self-supporting until just recently.

I've lived in Spokane since I was six, and never married, although I did have two kids, one when I was nineteen, the other at thirty. When I was eighteen I went to a community college, but that didn't lead to anything other than minimum-wage jobs working in places like fast-food restaurants.

Yet at the same time I always did some kind of volunteer work. For instance, I was working with the Catholic Church, helping out with religious education and youth services, coordinating youth nights and retreats.

And that led to the first job I ever had that paid more than minimum wage. I was named director of religious education at a Catholic church in the small town of Othello, Washington, the only time I'd ever been out of Spokane since childhood. I did that for two and a half years, and then decided to improve my lot by going back to school for a four-year degree, and then entered a master's program in social work.

Unfortunately, when I graduated, Spokane's job market was depressed, and there were more social workers here than positions open. So it looked bad for me again.

Then I heard about a position at AmeriCorps, which is a national volunteer project, a kind of domestic Peace Corps; they had a grant from Campus Compact, another national organization that helps promote service learning on higher-education campuses, earmarked for someone to work as a service-learning coordinator, which means running a program in which students perform service for a not-for-profit agency as an experiential component of their coursework.

I heard about it through a former professor whom I knew through the advocacy work I'd done during grad school for low-income people and welfare recipients. (I saw her at a function and made a joke about being unemployed six months after graduation.) She told me about this position, and I applied for and got it.

It was a volunteer post with a living stipend of $650 a month. I was still living in subsidized housing; I couldn't have afforded the job otherwise. Then I ran into some real luck. Service learning became so popular on campus that the faculty convinced the administration to make the position a full-time staff job. I applied. And, as the only applicant with prior service-learning experience, I was hired.

I can't tell you why I've always volunteered, even when I had nothing. Perhaps it's because things have been so rough for me in the past that I know where other people are coming from. Food stamps saved my life. So did the financial aid I received. Volunteers shouldn't just come from among the wealthy. They should be everyone.

*9. Sometimes the most valuable key to a successful career is someone wise and senior who becomes a role model. These sage advisers can be hard to find, but by volunteering and expanding your horizons, you'll increase the likelihood of meeting one.*

A mentor's function is to inspire you to believe in your self-worth and to help you realize your full potential. The mentor can be of practical help as well—opening doors, providing insights into your management style, helping you understand how a particular career path works.

In many organizations mentoring is a fact of life, and people who rise to the top are often pulled along by someone older and more senior. (This has been one of the many difficulties that women have to face in the business world, because there are fewer senior women to mentor younger ones. But as more women break through the "glass ceiling," that should change.)

Without question, my career path has been heavily influenced by a man I've looked to as a role model, John Whitehead. John was the first person I approached when I took the job running Outward Bound. John, who has a philanthropic bent, had already been involved in Outward Bound as a board member; in fact, I first met him when I was on the Outward Bound board myself.

Telling him I had to restaff, but without a budget, I asked for $100,000 a year for three years to do so.

"I'm willing to bet on you," John said. That was such an enormous vote of confidence—this money was coming directly out of his own pocket—that I felt a kind of confidence rare when you're working for a struggling organization. I knew with that support, I wouldn't fail.

Over time, as I watched John run his career, he carved out the formula already mentioned: spending one third of his time on volunteer organizations, another third working on outside boards, and the last third on his career. It's a formula that, as best I can, I've adapted to my own life.

I also tried to emulate John's management style. He was very quiet, very competent, with a twinkle in his eye; he never criticized anyone, he always emphasized the positive. He enjoyed receiving feedback and was constantly asking others their opinion. And he was very giving of himself, despite the tremendous pressures on his time—he always made time for people like me, and for organizations such as the Boy Scouts of America, of which he was chairman. No matter what he was doing, John made you think he *wanted* to spend time with you; even when others were lined up at his door, the last thing you'd ever see was John looking at his watch. He was focused on you, and you alone.

Finding such a mentor is a rare and memorable moment in anyone's life. Increase your chances. Leave your immediate circle. Meet outstanding people. Volunteer.

Actually, mentoring has become a prominent part of volunteerism itself. The most recent example: In Philadelphia on April 27, 1997, the President's Summit for America's Future brought together four previous U.S. presidents, hundreds of corporate CEOs, and thousands of volunteers at all levels to address the challenge of giving disadvantaged young people a better chance for a productive future in America.

One of the five basic goals at this conference, which was led by General Colin Powell, was to recruit, train, and put in place two million mentors for young people by the year 2000.

The conference was organized by Ray Chambers, a businessman and philanthropist dedicated to helping the young. After making a substantial fortune in venture capital, Ray founded the One to One Foundation, of which I was privileged to be a founding board member. One to One's mission is to generate mentoring, primarily through corporate sponsorship and by encouraging corporate employees to become mentors. Hundreds of corporations have signed on.

One to One is a catalyst organization, seeking to provide mentor candidates for existing mentor organizations, such as Big Brothers Big Sisters of America. To date, One to One programs have been established in Philadelphia, Boston, Minneapolis, and New York. So it works both ways when you volunteer. You can volunteer to mentor someone else, or if you're lucky, you can meet a mentor while you volunteer. Either way, you win.

## ABBIE DOROSIN'S STORY

When I was growing up I figured my career would involve helping people or animals, like being a doctor or a veterinarian. In high school I was a candy striper, and during college I was a counselor for kids and peers.

But after college I went in another direction. I took a job in an investment-banking firm, specifically working with a group that managed people's money. My interest in this job surprised me, my family, and my friends, but I was completely taken by what I was doing—primarily dealing with high net-worth individuals as well as corporate cash management. I liked the fast pace, the variety, and the challenge.

But the urge to volunteer was still there, so even though I didn't have a ton of time, I joined Community Impact, a not-for-profit that plans weekend volunteer projects for people who don't want to or can't make regular commitments. It sounded perfect. And once in a while, whenever I could, I'd spend a Saturday clearing a trail or painting a women's shelter. I liked the way Community Impact worked—the sense of community and the people involved, both the volunteers and staff.

Meanwhile, my interest in my job was waning; basically, I was getting burned out, and I decided to leave after eight years, without having another position lined up.

Once I had left, I did some job and informational interviewing and realized I was interested in a people-oriented rather than a product-oriented job.

During the same period, I became more involved as a volunteer staffer with Community Impact. Through that work I met a woman who had her own fund-raising and resource-development consulting firm for not-for-profit organizations. She was searching for an associate, and given that I was looking for something involving people, finance, and community-oriented work, it seemed like a perfect fit. I joined the firm, and have liked it ever since. I was happy to be part of a team doing something that makes a difference in the community, versus what I was doing before.

What do I do now? I spend most of my time fund-raising and doing community outreach for an organization whose mission is to bring people from different sectors together to act on issues affecting the economic vitality and quality of life in Silicon Valley.

The only downside has been the change in salary but, overall, when I factor in my quality of life, job satisfaction, and the people with whom I'm working, I am sure I made the right decision.

One of the things that makes all this worthwhile is my relationship with my boss. I've learned so much from her about running a small business: the nuances of understanding the client, paying attention to detail, learning to listen, building alliances, making judgments about where to spend time, and being savvy about resources, whether time or people or computer equipment.

The best part is that my boss showed me how to put our shared values—a belief in honesty and integrity, as well as balance between our professional and personal lives—into a business operation. I learned that these concepts aren't antithetical to the workplace; now I get to see them put into play every day. I hadn't been sure I'd find a boss with these values, but I did, and I'm very glad.

## LUKE O'NEIL'S STORY

After graduating from Georgetown Law School in 1984, I went north to Greenwich, Connecticut, to practice corporate law for a large New York City–based firm. Fortunately, the firm allowed me to continue my work with kids in the juvenile courts on a pro bono basis—work I'd started in law school. In addition, I signed on to be a Big Brother to an eleven-year-old named Hansel and began volunteering at the Boys & Girls Club.

Four years later, I woke up one morning and decided that the Boys & Girls Club needed someone with my skills to give 100 percent of his time and effort. So I jumped out of my suit and into a windowless, cockroach-infested office as the Club's associate executive director, and although I was working longer hours than at the law firm, I was working with kids every day and having the time of my life.

A few years later I took a course at Outward Bound; not long afterward they asked me to become an instructor, and soon I went to work for them in various positions for a few years. Outward Bound impressed me so much that I decided to start an educational community based on some of its principles. But I didn't have the right skills, so I enrolled at Harvard Business School to learn more about organization and finance.

While there, I decided to bring some of Outward Bound to the business school and, as a volunteer, was able to help revamp the school's orientation, making it a more user-friendly experience for new students, who before had been mostly just cursing their way through the first week. There we were, learning about service management, but we weren't doing such a good job of delivering it.

Through this volunteer work I met the school's dean. He seemed to take to me, and so I told him about my dream of starting an Outward Bound-style high school. He liked my ideas, and soon became my mentor, leading me to numerous people who could prove helpful. Many of them are now on my board.

As a mentor, he tells me when I'm going astray, and when I've got things right. He pushes me to focus on the big picture as well as on the nuts and bolts. Most of all, he believes in me; he sees my good qualities, and also sees those things in me that can become better over time. He makes me think through what I need to do to discover these qualities in myself.

Most amazingly, my mentor never tells me the right answer. He gives me clues and introduces me to the people and experiences that will allow me to learn the right answer on my own.

The school we're starting is called the Shackleton Schools, named after the great British explorer Sir Ernest Shackleton. It's based on the concept that some kids do best when enrolled in a learning community rather than the traditional school model. One example is Gordonstown, in England, where the students actually run the school. There they teach certain skills we don't teach here anymore—about being leaders, about inspiring others to go beyond what they think they're capable of doing. My dream is to re-create that kind of school in America.

*10. The strange and unforeseen can happen when you volunteer. You can grow in ways you've never considered, you can meet people you never knew existed, or, as in the following case, you can work for an organization that changes your life—and your career.*

Whenever you enter uncharted territory, you become unsure where your path may lead. Volunteer work certainly qualifies as uncharted territory because it seldom comes with the detailed job descriptions that accompany a traditional position. You can end up in places and roles you never dreamed possible. I don't think I've ever seen a volunteer organization that didn't allow for at least a small amount of constructive chaos in its ranks.

Hopefully, these surprises will all be pleasing, and I know of many stories in which volunteers went traveling off to places they never imagined, or found an old friend from childhood, or learned a valued new skill.

But sometimes the surprise can be that the organization you've joined is so special, so different from anything you've known before, that it changes your entire life.

Human Service Alliances (HSA) is one of these unusual places. Founded in 1986 and located in Winston-Salem, North Carolina, HSA is a not-for-profit, all-volunteer program that has affected the lives not just of those who receive its care, but those who volunteer to do its work.

Now over three hundred volunteers strong, HSA was established by a group of about twenty people who wanted to provide care for the terminally ill. The concept was to set up an organization where no one, neither staff nor administration, would receive any form of monetary compensation, letting the focus shine on the service.

A dozen years later, HSA still carries no paid staff while it works in four primary areas: care for the terminally ill, respite care for families with developmentally disabled children, a mediation project, and a health and wellness project. Over the last decade it's won a number of awards, including the Sara Lee Foundation National Community Service Award, and it was named one of President Bush's Thousand Points of Light. In 1995, HSA logged more than 60,000 hours of service, the equivalent of having a staff of 30 full-time employees.

Besides serving its community, because of its unusual nature HSA has inadvertently served its volunteers. It has, says cofounder LeAura Alderson, changed the way they think about their paying jobs: "We've learned the value and results of cooperation, even if it seems to be at personal expense. Being able to cooperate to help achieve a larger vision has made us all better employers and employees, since we're not fighting only for what we believe in, but for what the group believes in, just as we do at HSA."

Seminar leader Sanford Danziger says it's changed his professional life:

"Before, when running a seminar, I was interested in how I was coming across. In other words, I was interested in me. I've since learned to concentrate on how I can serve other people."

Sanford first heard of HSA while he was living in Arizona, and decided to move to North Carolina to join it. Other volunteers have come from all five continents, traveling at their own expense, to work with HSA.

One of the most remarkable aspects of the group has been the positive change it's prompted in its volunteers' careers. A truck driver developed communication and management skills meeting and working with the public and with his wife (whom he met at HSA; she is a former director of retirement homes) started a luxury motor-coach business that creates tours and traveling opportunities for the elderly. Another woman left her full-time corporate job to work in a cooperative school. A barely employed massage therapist went on to become a full-time employee in a chiropractor's office, with a successful massage business on the side. Another woman started her own business as an offshoot of the HSA health and wellness project.

Here are just two of the many such experiences from HSA:

## SUSAN BEASLEY'S STORY

Although I was a music major, after college I went to work for a law firm, and from there I held a variety of jobs until I decided to return to school for a degree in business administration and accounting. After all, if I was going to work for a living, I wanted a degree I could make money from.

I then worked in corporate accounting for several years. Who knows? I could have stayed there.

But even though I'd met my career and financial goals, my life seemed without any focused purpose. That's when I became aware of my deep inner urge to serve others.

So I started volunteering at a local hospice, going to people's homes, relieving family members so they could run errands. The relationships established were meaningful, and yet there was still something missing, something deeper.

Then, in 1986, I was fortunate that a friend invited me to a place where volunteers were caring for a terminally ill person in someone's home at no charge; this was the group of volunteers that eventually came together as Human Service Alliance.

I became more active in HSA over the years and eventually joined the board. No one on it was a CPA. I thought, why not me, then? Encouraged by the other volunteers, I took and passed the CPA exams. So basically I became a CPA to better serve.

I'd thought about getting the degree before, but it always seemed like too much work, and I hadn't wanted to study anymore. And studying really did turn out to be hard. But being a CPA has been great for my career—it's much better than the corporate accounting I was doing before. I have more flexibility, and I make as much money as I did before, but most important, the potential to make more is there, but whether to is my decision, not some boss's.

The other plus is that I've brought into my professional life a genuine interest in service, placing it in front of any personal agenda I might have. One of the lessons I've learned from volunteerism is to leave your ego at the door. And that carries over to my accounting. I find that when my clients come in and talk about what they need, I don't just automatically see pictures in my mind of how to answer them. I'm much more open to serving them as individuals. In other words, I know I'm just a vehicle, someone with specific skills they can use, rather than an ego that says, I know about taxes and this is what you have to do.

My clients may or may not see what I'm doing, but I know that it's working, because I'm getting wonderful feedback, and clients are sending me their family members and friends, and that's why my practice keeps growing.

# THOMAS WHITE'S STORY

After graduating from law school, I went on to become your basic small-town trial lawyer, doing a little bit of everything that involved going to the courtroom.

Then, in 1987, I started volunteering for a project for the terminally ill, which eventually became part of HSA. This changed the way I thought about volunteer work. Then, when HSA decided to initiate a mediation project, my career changed, too.

A mediator assists people in resolving conflict—something that might otherwise become a court case, such as a dispute over driveway rights, or a barking dog; anything major or minor that might be solved with the assistance of a third party.

Doing mediation got me involved with domestic relationship cases, divorces, property settlements, and so on. Some of these cases involved millions of dollars. And, at the other end of the spectrum, there was a woman who showed up in a taxi; she thought her case would take so little time and effort she had the driver leave the meter running.

At this point—the late 1980s—there was little mediation in North Carolina or anywhere else in the country. But people began to consider it a viable alternative to the clogged court system, so in 1992 the state government decided to experiment with several judicial districts, assigning them mandatory mediation programs with the intention of taking them statewide if things went well. Fortunately, since my county was among the pilot districts, I became one of the first state-sanctioned mediators.

In 1995 the program went statewide, and it's provided me with the capacity to move from being a litigator into being a full-time mediator. So I'm no longer a lawyer in the traditional sense.

I like this because it's such a natural progression. I'd spent twenty years working with people in adversarial positions. Now I've moved to a higher turn of the spiral, assisting those same types of people in resolving their conflicts by looking at common interests and goals. It's wonderful to see people analyze their needs and demands for the first time. Do I need to be so emotionally polarized, they ask themselves, or can I take a more thoughtful approach? People learn how to resolve conflict rationally and peacefully for the first time in their lives.

Once I was mediating a case where a family was arguing over the estate of a deceased father-stepfather. The stepmother, the surviving wife, and the various children all wanted their share, so they fought. During the course of mediation, each discovered that the others had real respect for the deceased, and when they realized this, they not only worked things out, they set aside some money to establish a scholarship fund in his name. Court procedure certainly doesn't allow for that sort of resolution.

One other thing: I'm fifty-four. A lot of people in their fifties are starting to look toward retirement; they feel they're in the twilight of their career. Not me. Retirement feels like something other people do. I'm starting a new profession in my fifties. That's exciting.

*11. There are many, many more advantages to being a volunteer. You may find your health improving, your self-image flourishing, your company thriving, and your relationship with your family changing for the better. Of course, all this is good for your career, too.*

Having worked in the executive-recruiting field, I can tell you that, although money is an important motivation, many people want to change jobs because they sense a lack of further opportunity, or because they're overwhelmed by the internal politics around them, or, most of all, because they're not feeling recognized or appreciated by their organization.

When you're out doing good works, however, you're participating in something that you've decided to do on your own, not something that someone else instructed you to do. This means you have a chance to feel both recognized and appreciated, since this is work motivated by your own heart, rather than someone else's bottom line.

When this happens, you're earning something that is as important as money, something that I've always thought of as psychic income. It's the feeling that comes from helping—a feeling of joy that is often very hard to come by in the business world. Joy—when you're caring for someone else, when you're giving back.

And why does this affect your career? Because that sense of joy accompanies you back to your workplace. You become a changed person. You feel good about yourself, and people enjoy being in the presence of someone who radiates a sense of inner happiness.

Furthermore, you stop deriving your sense of identity solely from your career. Few jobs will ever provide the kind of recognition and appreciation requisite to the human condition. But good works will.

Don't underestimate the power of psychic income. Someone whose life is rich in money but impoverished in self-worth is likely to face road blocks in his or her career. Throughout my years in business I saw so many men and women of promise fall by the wayside because they didn't take time to tend to their emotional lives. It isn't enough to land the big promotion, the great client, the terrific assignment. You also need to nurture your soul.

Volunteerism provides multiple means of gaining psychic income. For instance, many people tell me that their most important goal is to do their job competently and thoroughly, with enough time left over for family.

The answer? Even though you can't bring your children to your regular job, you often can bring them to your volunteer work. Or even better: You can volunteer together.

One friend tells the story of how his life was unraveling because of his long hours at the office. His wife was always angry, and his nine-year-old daughter picked up on that anger and returned it to him in odd ways. My friend had always been involved in charitable work, but he decided to switch from his previous activity, which was fund-raising for a large national organization, and instead became involved with his local PTA.

There he started working on small projects that he could do with his daughter and wife, including selling cookies door-to-door and raising money for a new school gymnasium.

The resulting work brought him and his family closer; my friend's work life stopped suffering so much from his unhappy home life and, to his surprise, his bosses noticed. "You were such a drag before," one of them said.

And from my own experience: Many years ago I was conducting a safety review at one of the Outward Bound programs in Oregon for what we then called Youth at Risk. These were unmanageable sixteen-year-olds heading for real trouble: They weren't attending school, they were experimenting with drugs, their lives seemed off-kilter.

I was waiting with many of the parents at the end of the difficult three-week course, which culminated in a nine-mile run. The parents hadn't seen their kids for weeks, and many were apprehensive about the results: Had their children changed? Did the program help? Did it make things worse? Because many of these parents saw the course as their last resort, the anxiety level was high.

I remember one parent in particular, a tough, solid man in his mid-fifties. It was early in the morning and chilly. His hands were shaking, so I asked him if he wanted some coffee.

"No," he said. He wasn't trembling because of the cold. He was just so full of trepidation and hope that he and his son might be able to get off to a fresh start.

When the kids finally appeared, many talked to their parents with an enthusiasm that the parents later told me they hadn't seen for a long time—in fact, many of them said that this was the first time their child had been open to them at all in years.

Parents and kids alike sat with staff members all day long, negotiating new norms of behavior: What was an unacceptable, or a red-light area; what was a negotiable, or yellow-light area, and what was an acceptable, or green-light area. The kids were agreeing to change, and the parents were too, for they had as much to learn about communication as their children.

It occurred to me that it was time I, too, changed the way I dealt with my own kids. I began to try being more tolerant, more open. I'd always been very demanding with my children, yet at the same time somewhat aloof, and this combination wasn't good. I was a tough taskmaster. So were many of the parents I was meeting, and it clearly hadn't been working for them, either.

For the first time I tried opening real lines of communication with my children, accepting their priorities and their manners, which weren't necessarily in line with mine.

Once my mind opened to this kind of thought pattern, I saw that I could change the way I worked with employees, too. I was often distant and cold at work. Now I decided it was time I stop demanding that everyone meet my own definition of success, and instead learn more about what others wanted from life, and from their careers.

The people I worked with noticed the change. I turned into a better parent and a better employer.

Personal growth is just one of the ways good works can pay you psychic income. Here are a few more:

An increasing amount of scientific research has established a strong link between good health and volunteerism. For instance, one recent study of 2,700 men in Tecumseh, Michigan, found that those involved in regular volunteer work had death rates two-and-one-half times lower than those who didn't volunteer. Further research at the UCLA and Harvard medical schools has supported this finding.

Among others who have studied the relationship between volunteerism and health are Dr. Bernie Siegel, author of *Love, Medicine and Miracles,* who has written extensively about the link between altruism and health, and George Vaillant, whose work at Harvard University monitoring the progress of a group of graduates over forty years has identified altruism as one of the factors that helps people overcome stress and improve the quality of their lives.

According to Douglas M. Lawson, Ph.D., author of *Give to Live,* many other studies have shown that volunteerism can result in a wide array of personal benefits, including greater longevity, increased self-acceptance, and reduced inner stress and conflict.

For years I've been saying that volunteerism can do so much good, but here is one finding that surprised even me. A carefully controlled study, recently published in the journal *Child Development* and conducted by an associate professor of psychology at the University of Virginia, found a pregnancy rate of 4.2 percent among 283 girls who participated in the National Teen Outreach Program throughout high school and did not enroll in sex-education classes. This program consisted mostly of community service, and it provided little to no information regarding birth control.

In contrast, a group of girls who did take the regular health and sex-education classes and did not volunteer in the outreach program had a pregnancy rate of 9.8 percent.

The study then concluded that teenage girls are less likely to become pregnant when their work for others helps them realize they are autonomous, caring individuals.

Furthermore, 27 percent of a selection of both boys and girls failed at least one course during their volunteer work, while 47 percent of those not doing volunteer work failed at least one course.

Another example: For the last two years, under a grant from the Ford Foundation, Benjamin A. Barber has been studying the effect of volunteer work on students. More than 1,700 volunteers have been tested at twenty-three national sites, and according to preliminary findings, students involved in volunteer activity tested much better in many areas than those not involved, including effectiveness in achieving goals, listening skills, public-speaking ability, knowing whom to contact in order to get things done, and the ability to compromise. All of these are important skills in the business world, and all were heightened by volunteer work.

Besides being good for your career, your body, and your soul, volunteerism is good for your company. In a study of 188 companies performed by Columbia University Business School, employee morale was three times greater in those firms with a high degree of community involvement than at uninvolved companies. Still another study in the 1980s by the Business Roundtable, chaired by Reginald Jones, former chairman and CEO of General Electric, showed that companies heavily involved in good works grew three times faster than the domestic GNP over the same period.

According to this study, if people had invested $30,000 in a composite of the Dow Jones index thirty years ago, it would be worth $134,000 today. If they had invested the same $30,000, putting $2,000 in each of the study's fifteen community-active companies instead, today their $30,000 would be worth more than $1 million.

Similarly, says James Burke, chairman of Johnson and Johnson, "Companies that organize their business around the broad concept of public service . . . provide superior performance for their stockholders."

# BILL JACOBSON'S STORY

I've been an entertainment lawyer in Beverly Hills for more than twenty years. I like what I do, but a few years ago I became aware that something was missing. I felt I'd run into some kind of emotional wall, and I didn't like the feeling. I needed to do something for myself. I wasn't sure what.

Then I remembered that years earlier I'd volunteered for a Saturday afternoon homeless feeding program, and it had made me feel pretty good about myself. So I thought I'd look around for something that would help others and also keep me interested in my life in a way that Beverly Hills law couldn't.

One of my son's friends was working as a student coach at Palisades High School, where they were busing in kids from the inner city. These were great kids. In order to arrive at school by 7:30, they had to get up at 5:30, and that's not easy for anyone. I figured if they would do that, *I* could drive the thirty minutes it took to get to the school from my office.

So I volunteered to coach the Pali High offensive linemen; I'd played football in high school and at college, but more than that, I thought I could help the kids get into college themselves.

When I first showed up, a lot of the seniors saw their high school graduation as the end of their education. They came from poor homes and felt an obligation to work; their parents hadn't gone to college, and they couldn't afford to send their kids, either.

Now, none of these kids had the physical ability to play Division I football. But if they worked hard, I told them, they might be able to get into a small-college program, which was something they'd never considered, since in L.A. the tendency is to think only about UCLA, USC, or their opponents. But small-college coaches are always looking for minority students from big-city football programs. I told these kids that if they could get a B average and play football well enough throughout the season, I would help them get into a small college.

It worked. While these small colleges don't give athletic scholarships, they do provide scholarships based on need, and many of the kids received good aid packages.

Once they were committed to the college, it was their choice whether they wanted to continue playing ball. As far as I was concerned, a degree was the goal, and football just the means. A couple of years ago one of my kids and his mom came back after his sophomore year to thank me. She added, "You always said, 'Use football to get into college, but once you get in there, it's not about football, it's about an education.' Well, he listened to you, and he's no longer playing football. The coach told him if he wanted to play, he needed to practice more, but he decided that he'd rather study and become a teacher."

"Great choice," I said to the kid. "You're never going to be a pro, but you'll make a great teacher."

In order to coach, I had to leave my office three or four days a week. So instead of going out to a fancy expense-account lunch, I'd go over to practice—I could still get work done on the car phone. Then I'd be back at the office at 4:30, a lot more refreshed than if I'd spent the time having a steak and a few drinks.

But the volunteer work meant more than feeling refreshed. Coaching changed my attitude toward my career. I hadn't been enjoying my practice—the routine of coming in, doing my work, going home—all of it had made me feel bleak. The problem was that I'd been relying on my job to provide a larger sense of fulfillment, and it couldn't do that. But the coaching could. I could see the effect I was having on these kids, and it made me feel needed. That attitude colored my life and my career.

The bottom line: During those years I volunteered at the school I made more money than I ever had before. And because I felt so good about myself, I felt great about my practice again. My attitude improved, my work improved, my practice improved. There was no question about it. I had a renewed sense of purpose in my life, and I can't think of anything that can improve a career more dramatically than that.

Before we end this chapter, I'd like to relate two more very personal stories. Neither of these explicitly concerns careers. Instead, each emphasizes the unexpected results and the unexpected pleasures of volunteerism.

Elizabeth Ratcliff is a grandmother and retired school teacher from Berkeley, California, who took a sightseeing trip to Washington, D.C., in 1986.

There she visited all the great war memorials, but when her vacation was over, she realized she hadn't seen anything expressing our country's allegiance to maintaining peace in the world.

"All our young people come by the millions with their families or teachers to Washington to see all the monuments to the sacrifices our people have made in war," she says. "But there should be something to balance this—something beautiful, for peace."

Elizabeth decided to dedicate her life to the creation of a national monument to serve as a constant and inspiring reminder to citizens and future peacemakers that the bedrock of democracy is a commitment to peace.

For almost a decade Elizabeth worked tirelessly to turn this dream into a reality, receiving support from several prominent politicians, including George Miller, a local representative who helped bring the idea to Congress; Dale Bumpers, the former senator from Arkansas; and a slew of consultants and architects. She spoke at innumerable rallies around the country, canvassed supermarkets and churches, and began to garner strong grass-roots support. She envisioned the monument as a garden rather than the typical federal building or statue, and worked to find support for that idea.

Finally, she made a successful appearance before Congress, which passed a bill establishing the National Peace Garden Monument; President Reagan then signed it. Ten acres on Hains Point, near the Jefferson Memorial, were assigned to the garden, and the National Park Service agreed to operate and maintain the garden as a national monument.

Elizabeth now had to deal with all the bureaucratic intricacies of getting design approval from numerous agencies, but again her patience was great enough to overcome a process that has defeated the far more experienced. After several false starts, and one plan going as far as the last sign-off before being rejected, today the design is final, and Elizabeth is in the process of raising the fifteen million dollars needed to build the garden. She's confident that, having come this far, her monument to peace will be in place by the beginning of the twenty-first century. I am proud to say that I am assisting in this project as the president of the National Peace Garden Monument.

Here is one dedicated woman, struck by an idea in the middle of a sightseeing tour, who decided that she could make a lasting difference by creating a legacy for our children to enjoy for generations to come.

Another story: Back in the early eighties I met a seventeen-year-old from South Carolina in a ninety-day semester course at the North Carolina Outward Bound School. The semester course qualified students for college credit and included thirty days of outdoor adventure learning, a service project, and a cross-cultural experience in a foreign country.

He was a shy young man who seemed to lack self-confidence; he was reluctant to take the lead or voice his opinion.

Along with his nine fellow students, he journeyed to Mexico to climb the great volcanoes and participate in a service project in Mexico City. On this particular day, the group visited an orphanage run by Mother Teresa for severely developmentally challenged children. The volunteers were to spend the entire day caring for and playing with the children.

The staff assigned him to a five-year-old boy who lay in a crib, unable to feed or wash himself. After being introduced to each other, the two were left alone while the staff attended to other students and their children. Then, after an hour, a few staff members became concerned that minding the little boy would be too much for the young man, who had no experience with developmental difficulties, and they returned to the second-floor room to check on the pair.

There they found the crib and the room empty; the two were nowhere in sight. Before anyone had time to panic, however, someone looked out the room's large window and saw the young man sitting on a sunny bench in the courtyard, the boy lying in his arms, tears shining on both their cheeks.

The volunteer describes the experience this way:

"I came on the trip for the volcanoes, but I left with a heart full of memories of the children in an overcrowded orphanage. I will never forget holding the little boy, tears streaming down both our faces in a moment of recognition and unexplainable joy. I intend to return there after I prepare myself to serve in a long-term way."

Here was a seventeen-year-old boy from middle-class America, touched by that unexplainable joy of recognizing common humanity with such a small, vulnerable five-year-old. And the child, too, recognized the love that was emanating from the volunteer as he was held so tightly in his arms.

e e cummings once said, "We do not believe in ourselves until someone reveals that deep inside us something is valuable, worth listening to, worthy of our trust, sacred to our touch. Once we believe in ourselves, we can risk curiosity, wonder, spontaneous delight, or any experience that reveals the human spirit."

What better way to find out what is valuable inside of us than through helping others? Yes, good works can do wonders for your career. They can do wonders for your spirit, too.

Your life isn't just about making money, or winning power, or becoming famous. It's not about what you've accumulated at the end of the day. It's about the entire day. Because if the journey wasn't fulfilling, no matter the outcome, getting there probably wasn't worth it.

As I've told so many business school audiences, try to develop balance in your life. Work shouldn't be your sole purpose. Being singlemindedly directed toward your career means that you run the risk of becoming one-dimensional. You are your job, your job is you, and that's the beginning and end of your self-definition. If that's the case, when you no longer have that job, who are you?

I've known people who were so identified with their work that, after losing their job, they became completely lost. Their identities had been so tied to the office, to the work, to the prestige, to the paycheck, that the absence of these things took away their feelings of self-worth.

But when you grow a career, as well as accompany it with good works, you'll find ways to manifest your values system and your identity outside of the office. Through that self-expression, you'll be able to achieve real balance in your life.

I always urge my business school audiences, and anyone else who'll listen, to think about these issues all the way through their career. Anyone who becomes overly focused on marketing, or finance, or operations, will miss much of what life is really about.

Think about it. How many people on their deathbed have looked back on their life and wished they had spent more time at the office?

Peter Drucker, often called "The Father Of Modern Management," has commented that the old definition of philanthropy—doing something for others—is no longer the entire story. We do things for ourselves, too, when we give back. At the core of the American commitment to volunteering is that we develop our own spirit when we give. That makes us all better citizens, and as a result, the entire country becomes stronger, more robust, and more humane.

In more ways than we can ever know, we all stand a little taller when we help someone else.

## PART II

# MAKING GOOD WORKS
# HAPPEN FOR YOU

*One thing I know, the only ones among you who will be truly happy*
*are those who have sought and found how to serve.*

Albert Schweitzer

You've decided that you want to become involved in some good works. Terrific! This may turn out to be one of your best moves ever.

But wait! Don't just fall into the first organization or assignment that comes along. You probably didn't take the first job offered to you. In all likelihood you thought about your career carefully, and then thought about yourself carefully, too; next, you researched your options, talked to others, and eventually made an enlightened decision.

Follow the same steps when you're entering the volunteer world. If you're interested in working one on one with another person, why end up in a place that requires you to sit behind a desk all day? If you have strong feelings about administration, don't work for a place that operates through total anarchy. If your goal is to work a few hours a week, it doesn't make sense to volunteer at an organization that expects you to be available every day.

Before you start, reflect on your interests and your life. What traits do you want to emphasize? Which do you want to downplay? If you've always been a behind-the-scenes type of worker, maybe this is the time to look for a position that offers you higher visibility. Or, if you're tired of working with large groups of people, you might seek out a place where your contribution is working with one individual.

Think about the type of commitment you want to make, the cause itself, and the amount of time you'll have to spend. Analyze what you have to offer the organization, and why they would want you to be involved.

One of the nicer elements of good works is that so many organizations need your help. This means that the options are almost overwhelming, which in turn means that, as a potential volunteer, you've got the luxury of being selective—probably much more so than in your professional career.

Unfortunately, because this process is personal, I can't take you through it step by step. It's like matchmaking: All the rational thinking in the world can't compete with the chemistry you feel when you know something is just right. Choosing service work isn't an exact science. It's a jumble of subjective elements, comprising the causes you support, the parts of yourself you hope to bring into play, the ways in which you want to relate to other people, and the time you have available to give, to name only a few criteria. Only you know these variables, and it's possible that you haven't identified them yet.

Still, try to organize your thinking sensibly before making a choice. This chapter consists of various aspects to consider while defining your purposes and goals, as well as ways to formulate your service résumé.

The single most important piece of advice I can give is: Work from your heart as well as your head. In judging your priorities, indulge your subjectivity. This is a great time to shed your self-doubts and workplace-related fears and instead think up new ways in which to fulfill yourself. If you have strong passions, follow them. Acknowledge the enjoyment you get from exercising a particular skill or ability. Pay attention to your feelings about the type of environment you like best.

Just because you've spent your life working in one arena doesn't mean you have to stay there. In fact, this is a great time to experiment. A lawyer can but doesn't have to do pro bono legal work; he or she can also ladle soup in a soup kitchen. A nurse can become an environmental advocate. A marketing director can coach a basketball team. A banker can become a friendly visitor at a hospital. I have one friend who's spent his life working with numbers, so when he stepped up to volunteer, he decided to donate his time to a community drama center, where no one can solve a single integrated algebraic equation, which makes him very happy. As he says, if he wanted to spend more time with numbers, he could do that at the office.

Service gives us all a chance to tailor our activities in the most individual ways. In the process, we not only feel good about our tasks, we bring out the best in ourselves and share it with others.

The place to begin your search? Start by looking inward.

Some people decide on a cause or a role very easily. They care deeply about one or more problems or issues, and they feel an impulse to contribute in a specific way.

But many others have no particular cause or passion leading them to a choice.

If you're in the former group, you shouldn't have a problem finding the right place: You may already know people who share your interests, so you can ask them; if not, you can always check the phone numbers of the organizations that perform the kind of work you admire.

But if you're like most people and fit into the second group, disengage your logical mind a bit. Get subjective. What are your hobbies, what do you enjoy in your spare time? For me, it was the outdoors and working with young people, which is part of the reason I looked into Outward Bound as a potential place to serve. Not only did I get a chance to give of my time, but I did it in an environment that made me feel happy—what more could anyone ask?

Examine yourself. If you read nonfiction, what topics do you choose? What are your greatest pleasures? When you call your best friend for no particular reason, what do you talk about?

Keep following this train of thought. Think about what gets your engine going. When you're listening to the radio in the kitchen, which news stories make you turn off the running water so you can hear more clearly? What newspaper articles make you talk to yourself? Ask your friends which topics you complain about most. What was the subject of the biggest argument about current events you've had?

Experiment with different ways of thinking. First, take the obvious route, in which the sports-minded apply to the Special Olympics, Little League, or the Police Athletic League; or those interested in culture work with art or music or look to museums or galleries for opportunities. Some athletically minded people may want to get involved in social-service groups that run sports programs. Athletes who want to spend more time outdoors might apply to an environmental conservancy group or an outdoor adventure-based organization like Outward Bound.

But think about going beyond the obvious. Some athletes may want to emphasize other skills. Maybe this is the time to chuck your athletic identity and try out a new self-image as a thinker. Maybe everyone thinks you're a jock, but you've always had a secret interest in sculpture. Try it out.

Even after this kind of self-analysis, many people won't have a clue what type of good-works project is best for them. If you find yourself in similar straits, think about visiting a nearby volunteer center or a United Way office. The reason? There you can talk things through with someone experienced in the field, or simply watch others at work and see first hand what appeals to you. A staff member at one of those offices not only will help you in your search for a cause and a role, but will also be able to describe local organizations and their programs.

## THE ESSENTIAL YOU

If you're still stuck, here are more questions to help elicit some basic information about the essential you.

What is your motivation for doing volunteer service? If you want to go off on your own and contribute in a creative, personal way, don't become involved in an intense team effort that ties your actions inextricably with those of other volunteers. I knew one very independent woman who became part of a group team to work with urban HIV-infected men and women. She did excellent one-on-one work, but the program was organized so that every Monday the other volunteers on her team meet to talk about their progress.

My friend couldn't deal with that kind of enforced social participation. "I love working with my patient," she said, "But I can't stand sitting there and hearing all these other people talk for hours about what they're going through. It makes me feel sad, because I'd like to be interested. But the fact is, I'm not, and at the age of thirty-nine, I'm not going to change." She eventually found another organization for which she could do the kind of work she liked without having to participate in the other volunteers' lives.

If your motivation is personal growth, find a volunteer involvement that lets you experiment with your inner self. My friend Jack took a job for a large firm specializing in litigation right after graduating from law school, and he worked fourteen hours a day six to seven days a week for twenty years. Then he decided to angle for a judgeship, which he obtained, and all of a sudden he had more free time than he dreamed possible.

"It was time for me to learn more about myself," he said. "I hadn't had an introspective thought in two decades." Jack then volunteered to help a New Age–type of organization in San Francisco that needed legal assistance, and took several courses in everything from Eastern religion to pottery while he was there. "It's exactly what I needed," he said. "At the age of forty-seven all I knew about myself was that I was a lawyer. Now I'm beginning to expand that definition a little."

One cautionary note: People who have lost close friends or family members to illness sometimes volunteer for an organization related to that disease. However, lingering feelings of sadness or depression may still be hovering close to the surface, especially when the death has occurred recently. Don't forget, this is volunteer work. At your office you might not want to be so open about vulnerable areas in your life, but here you can and should let others know. Talk to someone on the staff candidly. And if you both decide that you're not ready to face the issue, then wait a little while. Work in another area, and then return when you're stronger.

Still, some of the best volunteer work I've ever seen was prompted by a serious illness that afflicted a family member. Judy Resnick, chairman of the Resnick Group, a money-management company in Beverly Hills and the author of *I've Been Rich. I've Been Poor. Rich is Better,* became actively involved with the Crohn's Disease Foundation. Crohn's disease is a serious inflammation of the lower part of the small intestine that causes chronic diarrhea, severe weight loss, and other unpleasant symptoms. No one knows what causes it, nor do they know how to cure it. But they do know it makes the sufferer feel completely dreadful. And Judy's daughter Stacey has had to deal with it throughout her life.

Judy says, "I remember a time when Stacey was extremely ill, facing an uncertain future, lying in bed with an IV. As a mother I felt so horribly helpless. So I decided to act. I educated myself about the disease and eventually was appointed to the board of the Crohn's Disease Foundation, where I quickly raised over $150,000. Becoming proactive didn't improve my daughter's health. It didn't cure the disease. But it made feel me better. I gained some knowledge and I lost some fear. And it also made Stacey proud of me, which helps us both."

In my family, my niece, Martha Anderson, was a bright and lovely Wellesley College graduate who went to India to make a difference. There, after falling extremely ill, she became the victim of adult-onset schizophrenia, and despite a valiant struggle with the disease, she took her own life several years later. Her mother, my sister Helen, sought to make Martha's devotion to making a difference live on by volunteering to work at The Schizophrenia Association of Minnesota. There she catalogued names, performed office work, and helped with fund-raising. Eventually she went on to become the association's president.

Here are some more questions to ask yourself: What kind of energy do you have? Do you have spontaneous reactions? Or are you the methodical, thorough type? Once you've had those two cups of coffee, do you work straight through without taking a break? Or are you someone who likes to put your feet up and let your mind wander every couple of hours?

Don't think about your career persona, or about the way you'd like to be, or even about the way you think you should be. Instead, think about who you are on weekends and work around that image: It probably says a lot more about who you really are.

Do you like to create ideas or implement existing ones? If you don't like taking orders, don't accept an assignment in a highly bureaucratized organization. Find a situation where your creative thinking will be a strength rather than a stumbling block. On the other hand, if you're a follower, don't let yourself get talked into running a workshop or chairing a committee.

Project yourself into the future. As with paid employment, entry-level jobs in the service world are sometimes just that. It's when a volunteer becomes established and makes a solid contribution that personal preferences are most respected. When you interview, inquire about the jobs that will be available *after* you're established.

Still more questions: What is your best method of relating to people? Do you prefer groups or one-on-one involvement? Do you like being with people for long periods of time, such as a day or a weekend, or for shorter periods? Do you need privacy, or are you happiest when surrounded by others? Do you enjoy a nice quiet chat, or are you at your best in a fast exchange of thoughts and ideas?

What keeps you going when the going gets tough? Is it approval and applause? Quiet feedback from other people? A sustaining belief in what you're doing? Do you need a lot of positive reinforcement on a regular basis, or can you go without it? People differ widely in the amount and kinds of support they require. While a fund-raiser may be rewarded by a small number of dramatic successes, a direct-service volunteer may find sustaining satisfaction in the smile of a child, or in the progress of someone he is tutoring.

What kind of environment is right (or wrong) for you? Be creative. Plenty of people are depressed by hospitals and nursing homes, and there's nothing at all wrong with that. But if you want, you can still work with people who are convalescing by avoiding institutional settings and investigating in-home visitation programs.

What about the outdoors? Check out sports or backpacking organizations, including those run by social-service agencies, or environmental groups involved with trail maintenance.

What are your passions? Do you love talking on the telephone? Think about investigating hot lines. Are you an amateur artist? Maybe your church needs someone to design its bulletin. Do you like kids? Consider the children's ward at the hospital or day-care center. Do you love cooking for others? Meals on Wheels could be just the group for you.

While you're thinking about these passions, don't forget your bêtes noires, too. Do you hate paperwork? Does physical suffering make you queasy? Do you faint at the sight of blood? Would you find it difficult to ask people for donations of money? I had a friend who once volunteered for a blood drive and spent most of his time on a couch, having passed out the first time a needle malfunctioned.

There's no point in bringing up your aversions out of context, but if you suspect that a particular assignment or task may create a problem for you or the organization, discuss it as early as possible.

Finally: Make a list of your strong points. Not all of them will be applicable to every situation, and in some situations some won't come into play at all, but be ready to bring them up if the situation suggests their usefulness.

## YOUR TIME SCHEDULE

Many groups ask for a commitment of time up front. This may seem somewhat aggressive to new volunteers, but it's a question of benefit to both the volunteer and the organization. The typical nonprofit staff devotes considerable time and effort to integrating people into the organization, and the volunteer devotes an equivalent amount of energy.

Realistically evaluate the demands on your time from any of the following:

- Your family. Allow ample time for small emergencies to crop up.

- Your career. This includes work you bring home from the office.
- Your schooling. Make sure you don't skimp on homework time.
- Your free time. Take into account the occasional business trip and weekend at the shore.

One trap to watch for is the temptation to substitute volunteer work for another area of your life that needs attention but that you find less satisfying. I see this happen often. For instance, my friend Gary's doctor told him that for health reasons he needed to lose a considerable amount of weight, but Gary decided that instead of going to the gym, which he hated, he'd use his time to work with cancer patients in a local hospital. Gary's inclination was admirable, but the choice simply wasn't appropriate for him—as they say, you also have to tend to your own garden.

Likewise, my friend Clara decided to let her kids skip their daily chores at home so they could tutor underprivileged children at a nearby church. This may have been a great learning experience for her kids, but it wreaked havoc on Clara's house and on her own schedule.

When evaluating your time, be realistic. Go back over your appointment book for the last few months and see what kind of time was truly free. Often we think we have more free time than we really do, because we forget how much of our day is taken up by routine chores that we can't remember doing—but that are essential to our lives. You may think you didn't do a thing last weekend, but the truth is you fixed the drains, washed the car, cleaned the back porch, took the dog to the vet, and so on. None of it may seem important, but your life would be far worse if you didn't take care of these things.

On the other hand, don't forget when looking over your schedule that you can substitute service work for current activity that isn't particularly fulfilling or necessary. Maybe you spend every Tuesday night at the bowling alley, but that doesn't mean you might not enjoy trading that time for something more satisfying. You may never bowl a perfect game, but you might help someone else land on his feet.

A final piece of time-related advice: Establish your availability beforehand rather than molding it to the particular needs of a group. Not that you should be inflexible—but knowing your best schedule in advance can make it easier for you to decide among the possible options.

## AN INVENTORY OF SKILLS AND ABILITIES

The lists below are intended to demonstrate the scope of skills that can be applied to volunteer work and also to help jog your awareness of your abilities: Trained or untrained, you may have more skills than you suspect.

Sometimes these skills may qualify you to contribute to an organization in a specific way: A person versed in advertising or architecture may be particularly needed by an organization. Then again, sometimes all that's needed is someone whose best skill is the basic ability to listen. Believe me, there can never be enough people like that.

Or, you may be called upon to teach or otherwise pass along your talents. A vocational training program may need someone with bookkeeping skills or a knowledge of auto mechanics. Personal qualities such as strength, wisdom, and maturity become almost tangible commodities when mentors provide role models for young people, or when retired executives advise fledgling businesses here and abroad.

However, go easy on yourself. You don't have to be a professional librarian to count library work as one of your skills, or a CPA to list accounting as an ability. This isn't a licensing examination. If you have reasonable exposure to and experience in an area, consider it part of your repertory. The depth of knowledge and experience required will come out in discussions with an organization's representative.

As noted, there is still another reason why volunteer work can be so complementary to your career: You can test out the skills you want to stretch but don't have the opportunity to use at the office.

While you inventory your skills, remember to focus only on the ones you really enjoy using. If you're great at crunching numbers but sick to death of figures, why volunteer to spend even more of your time working with them?

## SKILLS INVENTORY

Accounting
Administration
Advertising
Agriculture
Arbitration, mediation
Architecture
Audiovisuals
Auto mechanics
Banking
Bookkeeping
Braille
Brochure/newsletter preparation
Brokerage: financial, real estate
Budgeting
Bus driving
Carpentry
Cataloging
Clerical work
Clinic work
Collections
Computer programming
Computer training
Conference/workshop planning
Construction
Continuing education
Copywriting

Cost analysis
Counseling: personal, career, marriage, unemployment,
retirement, family, teenage
Crafts
Curriculum design
Dietetics
Direct mail
Dispatching
Drafting
Editing
Electronics
Energy conservation
Engineering: chemical, environmental, mechanical
Entrepreneurship
Estimating
Executive search
Family planning
Filing
Film production
Finance
First aid
Food service
Foreign languages
Grant/proposal writing
Graphic arts
Housing development
Insurance planning
Interior design, decoration
Interviewing
Inventory control
Investment planning
Journalism
Labor relations

Laboratory work
Landscaping
Law
Legal aid
Library work
Licensing, franchising
Long-range planning
Maintenance, janitorial work
Management training
Mapmaking
Market research
Marketing
Massage
Mechanical drawing
Medical technology
Medicine
Merchandising
Natural science
Nursing
Nutrition
Office systems
Operations management
Paralegal services
Payroll
Performing: music, drama, dance
Personnel management
Photography
Planning
Policy-making
Pricing
Printing, typesetting
Product display
Production

Program development
Project coordination
Promotion
Property management
Psychiatry
Psychology
Public relations
Public speaking
Purchasing
Real estate
Reception
Remedial reading
Research
Retail sales
Sales management
Sales representation
Science: research, application
Securities management
Small business administration
Social work
Speech therapy
Statistics
Stenography, transcription
Strategic planning
Systems planning
Tax counseling
Teaching
Teaching assistance
Technical writing
Telephone sales
Therapy, physical
Therapy, psychological
Time management

Tour guiding
Truck driving
Tutoring
Typing
Urban planning
Veterinary medicine
Videotape production
Word processing
Writing: advertising, business, creative

Something to consider alongside of skills are abilities: When you're thinking about what you can offer in volunteer work, aptitudes can be as important as real skills. This list was compiled with the help of many people who have served in good works—both volunteers and those who run programs:

## ABILITIES INVENTORY

Abstract thinking
Adaptability
Appliance repair
Analytical skills
Animal care
Art appreciation
Assertiveness
Attention to detail
Awareness of the big picture
Balance of idealism and realism
Bargaining
Brainstorming
Budgeting
Carefulness
Child rearing
Coaching individual sports
Coaching team sports

Comfort with strangers
Committee work
Communications
Community organizing
Companionship
Conflict management
Construction
Conversation
Cooking
Cooperation
Coordination: people, schedules, events
Courage
Crafts
Creative thinking
Crisis intervention
Decision-making
Demonstrating
Detail orientation
Dispute settlement
Emotional support
Empathy
Encouraging others
Establishing easy rapport
Event management
Exercise and physical fitness
Explaining things clearly
Follow-up
Foreign languages
Friendliness
Fund-raising
Gardening
Goal-setting
Good memory

Handling money
Hiking, backpacking
Hobbies: all kinds
Home repair
Homemaking
Hospice work
Hosting
Housecleaning
House painting
Imagination
Improvising
Independence
Insightfulness
Intuition about people
Inventiveness
Letter-writing
Listening
Logic
Machine operation
Machine repair
Martial arts
Mediation
Money management
Motivating others
Originality
Paperwork
Party-planning
Patience
Persistence
Physical strength
Problem-solving
Reading aloud
Record keeping

Recovery from substance abuse
Relaxation techniques
Religious education
Risk-taking
Schedule-making
Self-discipline
Self-motivation
Sensitivity to feelings
Sewing, dressmaking
Shopping
Signing for the hearing impaired
Sports: coaching, refereeing
Storytelling
Stress management
Supervising adults, children
Swimming
Theoretical thinking
Thoroughness
Travel
Trouble-shooting
Upholstery

## LOOKING FOR GOOD WORKS

Now that you've thought about your skills and abilities, and have decided how you want to participate and what parts of your character you want to draw upon, it's time to think about contacting organizations, and *how* you want to approach them. In other words, you're now ready to position yourself, just as you would for any job that interests you.

In describing yourself and the kinds of contributions you want to make, you are creating a personal profile to present to organizations and agencies. If you decide to look for a policy-making job, emphasize skills that involve planning and creating ideas. If you're interested in direct service, focus on your abilities to work well with people, as well as any practical skills that apply.

Start preparing a list of questions you'll want answered in interviews, and be ready to participate in those conversations in an active, investigative way. Find out as much as you can about the organization that interests you, especially as to how you might fit in. And when you see how the fit might be accomplished, share your insight. Don't be shy. Like people, organizations are most eager to connect with others who are right for them.

Your next major step will be finding an organization. Most people learn about good works through two basic routes: networking with friends and professional contacts, and investigating on their own.

## NETWORKING

Networking—learning about organizations through friends, family, and business and other associates—is one of the easiest and most reliable ways to investigate service organizations. When you know people, even if through a formal relationship as is often the case in business, you sense what's important to them; thus, their recommendations can be viewed through the prism of perceived biases and prejudices, both positive and negative.

Networking operates in dozens of ways. Perhaps you hear of an organization through a conversation with your cousin; maybe a friend at work urges you to attend a recruitment meeting or to come along on a direct-service assignment; or maybe you hear of something at a college reunion.

Probably my best volunteer work—at Outward Bound—came to me through my son Bill, who was a high school student in New Canaan when he told me he wanted to take one of the organization's courses; he asked if I'd be willing to come to his high school for a briefing.

The man giving the meeting, Will Sawyer, was the vice president of development for Outward Bound and had been in the Navy SEALS in Vietnam. Since I'd been a member of a Navy underwater demolition team in Korea, I went up to talk to Will when the meeting ended to ask if he knew any of my Navy friends who'd stayed in the service and become SEALS; it turned out he did.

Not long afterward I was invited by the national Outward Bound organization to go on an introductory six-day whitewater rafting trip on the Colorado River for business leaders. I went and enjoyed it immensely. That, and some initial fund-raising I did, led the board to ask me to join them, which, as you already know, led to my becoming the organization's CEO— all because my son Bill wanted me to attend a lecture with him one night.

Networking often occurs this naturally, but you can also encourage it to happen. If your parents are, or were, involved in volunteering in the past, ask about their experiences. Ask your brothers, sisters, aunts, nieces, nephews, and so on. Whenever you know someone who's been working in an area that sparks your interest, get them to tell you more. You may be surprised by what you can pick up from friends and acquaintances. Maybe it's because volunteer work can be so personal, or perhaps because it's only a small part of someone's day, but many people go about their lives without ever mentioning their good works. In fact, you could be surrounded by people who are already deeply involved this moment, but you'd never know, since they've never told you, and you've never asked.

Another place to look: Many companies have community-service programs. Even if they don't have an official one, the public relations or human resources office may have information about groups the company works with informally. So if your corporation has these kinds of ties, some of your associates, as well as their spouses and children, are likely to be involved.

And, of course, if you belong to a religious organization, ask a staffer or other members about community service. Many churches, synagogues, and mosques will have a community-outreach program.

One important point: Don't be afraid to talk to people you don't know. In fact, since it usually means a great deal to them, once you bring it up you may not be able to stop others from talking about their good works. And because organizations are always looking for new members, established volunteers are generally delighted to hear from someone considering joining their ranks.

\*       \*       \*

Whether you're young and just starting your career, or newly arrived in a strange city, or have lived in one place all your life, network to find out about the best organizations available: the ones that are most active, the ones that are growing, the ones that do the most good. If you know a community leader or a board member of an organization that appeals to you, don't hesitate to call on that person for information and advice. He or she can be invaluable in introducing you to the organization and getting you involved.

There is one potential danger in the networking approach. Sometimes the enthusiasm of someone close to you can substitute for your own feelings for a cause or group. When a friend gets carried away about how much an organization means to him, enjoy that passion, but be careful. Let networking operate at full force in introducing you to groups and programs, but be sure your evaluation of them is entirely your own.

## ON YOUR OWN

Here are some organizations and other sources in your community that can provide direct or indirect help in your search for the service assignment that is right for you.

## VOLUNTEER CENTERS

Sometimes known as voluntary action centers, or volunteer bureaus, volunteer centers play the role of advocate and catalyst for volunteerism in their communities, providing education and support for volunteer efforts, and acting as central clearinghouses for local volunteer opportunities. More than 380 volunteer centers currently operate across the nation; almost all of the one hundred largest metropolitan areas have at least one. All told, these centers serve more than one hundred thousand private organizations and public agencies.

Center staff members can offer current information about the needs of local organizations and are trained to match volunteers with possible assignments, although final decisions are left to the individual and the organization in question.

To locate a volunteer center in your area, look in the White Pages of the telephone directory under Volunteer or Voluntary. If you can't find a listing, check the Yellow Pages under Social Service or Community Organizations.

## UNITED WAY OFFICES

United Way has 2,300 chapters located throughout the country. In addition to raising and allocating funds for other organizations, many United Way offices also serve as clearinghouses that match individuals with volunteer opportunities in the community.

## PUBLIC LIBRARIES

Libraries contain a number of helpful reference books you can use to research organizations that use volunteers. Ask a librarian for local or regional directories of nonprofit or social-service agencies. Also, your library probably carries the *Encyclopedia of Associations,* a multivolume directory of associations of all types, organized by category. Don't let its hefty size and multiple volumes intimidate you; it's self-explanatory, or the librarian can show you how to use it.

## MUNICIPAL OFFICES

Contact or visit the mayor's office, some of the various departments of your city or town hall, or a community center. Any of these is likely to have directories or lists of local service organizations, and you may get a few leads just talking on the phone or chatting with a clerk or police officer. Or, you can attend town meetings or city council meetings.

## YOUR LOCAL COURT AND CRIMINAL JUSTICE SYSTEM

More and more judicial systems are using volunteers in counseling and rehabilitation programs for young people and adults charged with and convicted of crimes. They are looking for volunteers; you can find the numbers in the Yellow Pages.

## LOCAL BUSINESSES

Chambers of commerce and other business and consumer councils, as well as individual manufacturers, merchants, bankers, and other professionals, will have opinions—often very strong ones—about community problems and issues and the best ways to approach them. If you're comfortable with your community's local business leaders, talking with them might be an excellent route to pursue to identify volunteer opportunities—or create some.

## LOCAL SERVICE CLUBS

Contact your local Kiwanis, Rotary, Lions, Elks, and other service clubs. Some local groups are mainly concerned with commercial good fellowship, but many others are involved in innovative social-service efforts. For instance, the Lions Club has taken on a national project to assist the blind, and Rotarians are active in sponsoring local scholarships.

## CHURCHES, SYNAGOGUES, AND MOSQUES

Even if you're not a member of a congregation, contact a couple of ministers, priests, or rabbis, any of whom will be excellent sources on what's being done in the community—and what needs to be done.

## SCHOOLS

Call or visit the administrative offices of the elementary and secondary schools, community colleges, and universities in your area. Attend school board and PTA meetings. If you are particularly interested in working in a school setting, arrange a meeting with a school counselor, principal, teacher, coach, or other official.

## WOMEN'S CLUBS

In many cities, women's clubs have a long record of voluntary assistance, and their representatives can guide you to any number of volunteer options. Contact your local women's club, Junior League, League of Women Voters, or women's business group.

## Hospitals and Nursing Homes

Institutions that care for ill and elderly people can always use volunteers for their programs. They're also a good source for learning about outpatient programs run by nonprofit groups. See the White and Yellow Pages; when you call, ask for the director of volunteer programs. If no such position exists, try the director of administration.

## Newspapers

Read your local print media, including neighborhood and shopping handouts, for write-ups on organizations and their activities. Read editorials as well as news stories. If you're after something specific, look for the bylines of reporters covering issues that interest you and give them a call.

## Television and Radio Stations

The broadcast media carry many public-service announcements and feature stories about people helping others or working for a worthy cause. Contact the station if you catch only the tail end of something that sounds interesting; ask someone to send you reprints of stories and editorials containing the necessary names and numbers.

## The Internet

Many, if not all large volunteer organizations have Web sites offering a plethora of information. Besides detailed specifics about each organization, the Net has links to so many other volunteer organizations that you could be busy for weeks tracking them all down.

For instance, http://www.servenet.org is an excellent place to start. Here you can find information about all kinds of volunteer organizations, read message boards, learn about other volunteers, and so on. You can also try visiting the stite of a national organization such as the Corporation for National Service, at http://www.cns.gov. CNS was chartered by Congress in 1993 to provide a broad range of local and national service opportunities to Americans of all ages. Another excellent site is the Internet Nonprofit Center, at http://www.nonprofits.org, where you can search for information on any nonprofit in any state.

## COMMUNITY BULLETIN BOARDS

Check the notices and ads posted at town halls, libraries, retailers, grocery stores, dry cleaners, laundromats—wherever bulletin boards exist in your neighborhood. One of my best friends once found a highly satisfying volunteer position by replying to an ad he spotted on a gym bulletin board seeking help for a Meals on Wheels operation.

## POLITICAL REPRESENTATIVES

The office of your elected officials—local, state, and national—can also be helpful in identifying volunteer work. Consider contacting both present and past political leaders and current candidates for public office. You can also try attending local political meetings for insights into local problems and ideas for private action.

## PERFORMING ARTS GROUPS

If you like the arts, approach local theaters and other cultural organizations. Sometimes all it takes is a walk to your local theater to ask if they need help—you'll find that whenever you offer your services for free, people are eager to talk to you.

## LOCAL MUSEUMS AND HISTORICAL SOCIETIES

Again, consult the White and Yellow Pages. While some local historical societies may be essentially one-man or one-woman operations, others will welcome offers of help.

## SENIOR CITIZENS CENTERS AND AGENCIES

Churches, local government offices, and the telephone book will direct you to these groups, which may simply provide the elderly with places to socialize or actually run numerous programs to support the lives of their members or clients.

## SOCIAL SERVICE AGENCIES

Public and private agencies of all kinds—serving children, families, the elderly, the unemployed, and many other groups—are listed in the telephone directory under Health and Welfare Agencies, Human Services, Service Organizations, Social Services, and similar headings.

## LOCAL BRANCHES OF NATIONAL ORGANIZATIONS

The directories found in your local library may tell you which national groups have local branches. If you live in a large city, consult your local phone book for this information. Using the *Encyclopedia of Associations,* you can also contact the main headquarters of national organizations to find the chapter closest to your town.

## SPECIAL AVENUES OF APPROACH

For students: An increasing number of high schools are making service a part of their curricula. Some are even requiring a certain number of community-service hours as a prerequisite for graduation. High school students should make their interest in volunteering known to a guidance counselor or the school administration; it may fit in with an existing or developing plan.

College students can contact their activities office or campus administration for leads. Be persistent; sometimes volunteer offices are new and, if part of a large university, may not yet have established many connections within the academic bureaucracy.

Students can also contact two relatively new and dynamic national organizations that promote student volunteerism: the Campus Outreach Opportunity League (COOL) and Campus Compact. One or both of these groups may be newly established on your campus; if not, interested students and faculty members can initiate opening a chapter.

For older people: Volunteer opportunities for senior citizens abound. Beyond the need for experienced people in almost all nonprofit groups, several large programs exist that specifically tap the talents of older people. A few examples are the American Association of Retired Persons (AARP); the Retired Senior Volunteer Program, run by ACTION, the federal domestic volunteer agency; the International Executive Service Corps; and the National Executive Service Corps.

## GETTING INFORMED

As you will see from exploring some of the avenues just mentioned, thousands of volunteering options are available. While it might be nice to spend time learning about every one of them before picking your course of action, that would leave no time to actually do the work. So think about narrowing your search to about half a dozen promising organizations. Then, collect printed material about each one before you contact them for interviews. Almost all groups publish some kind of handout describing their work; if you call to have information sent to you, be sure to state what part of the organization interests you so that they can send material tailored for potential volunteers in that area.

## EVALUATING ORGANIZATIONS

If you don't have the guidance of a friend or acquaintance to help you assess the groups you've selected, take the cold-call approach. If you can, ask for a director of recruitment, or the director of the volunteer program. If no such person is available, contact the office of the executive director. Say that you're interested in the organization and would like to learn more about its work and how you might fit in.

Position yourself by describing the kind of contribution you feel you can make. Bear in mind your reflections on the essential you. Know how you feel about the cause. And know which of your skills and abilities—developed or yet-to-be-exercised—you want to emphasize. Besides answering the usual questions that will come your way, be sure to create opportunities in the conversation to mention what you have to contribute.

Whether you make the contact through networking or your own investigating, you'll eventually be asked to come in for an interview, whether it's an informal chat over coffee or an appointment at the offices of the organization. Remember, you have two agendas. One is to present yourself honestly to members of the organization, so they can best decide how your skills might fit their needs. The other is to evaluate *them*. Eagerness and enthusiasm sometimes propel people into joining a group before they really know enough about it to make an enlightened decision. Please, read and think carefully about the nonprofits you are considering.

## POINTS TO PONDER

The following questions are offered to guide your thinking.

What is an organization's mission and philosophy? Do you agree with it? Sure, you say, why else would I be interested? Well, you may have a preconception about a group that could later prove to be wrong. You may think you're interested because a friend is, but when you hear about the group's goals from a third party, they may not sound on-target for you. You might still agree with the general aim of the group, but not their specific approach to it.

For instance, several years ago I became interested in a prison-visiting service program through a friend. It seemed tailor-made for my time and energies: It sounded as though I could work with some young man during his years in prison, and at times convenient to my schedule.

But when I went through my first interview, I discovered that volunteering with the program meant working with not one, but five prisoners, and the prison population with which they wanted me to work was all-female. I didn't feel capable of giving these women the type of support they needed; I felt more adept at working with young men. So I decided that although the program was completely commendable, it just wasn't what *I* was looking for.

More questions: How is an organization supported? Each person will have his or her own views on what's appropriate. Some may want to avoid organizations that are sponsored, even in part, by government or corporations. Others may want to steer clear of groups with religious ties or political orientations. And some won't care at all about the source of a group's money.

How does this group relate to the community? With what other local groups in the community does it have ties? How are volunteers and board members recruited? Who are its paid staff? Is fund-raising done locally? How does the group benefit the community? If the organization has clients, who are they? What are the special characteristics of the client population, the needs or problems that bring them to this agency?

What is the structure of the organization? What is the proportion of paid staff to volunteers? How is the organization structured? Is it well managed? Who's really in charge? Can you even tell? How are the large decisions made? What about small decisions: Are approvals needed at every step, or is there relative freedom to act?

How dynamic or innovative is the group? (One way to check is to ask for a brief, casual history of the group's activities within the past two or three years.)

What is expected of the volunteers in general? What's expected of *you*? What are the responsibilities involved? What are the personal qualities that are required for performing a particular task? (If they can't tell you, it's a bad sign.) How much decision-making is expected or required of volunteers?

Is there a volunteer-training program, or are volunteers used on an informal basis? Your experience in an organization with a formalized program will be different in some ways from working in a group that uses volunteers on an ad hoc basis, or one that hasn't developed formal training programs and methods of managing assignments.

What kind of training is provided? Is it formal or informal? Is it one-on-one or offered in workshops, classes, and seminars? Is it accomplished through lectures, case studies, role playing? What topics are covered? How much training is offered and how much is required?

Is there ongoing supervision, guidance, and support for volunteers? Some organizations provide in-person and telephone consultations, buddy systems, group meetings, periodic conferences, and workshops. If there's no formalized support mechanisms, will there be open access to staff members? Be sure you understand the lines of communication, because you'll depend on them.

What are the possibilities for taking greater responsibility? In other words, what are the chances for advancement? Even if you don't think you want to be a committee chair or board member, it's good to know whether the organization welcomes new blood circulating upward through its ranks. What are the criteria for board membership? Is simply having deep pockets enough?

And, of course, after asking about all this, ask yourself: Are you still interested in volunteering?

## WHAT TO DO AFTER AN INTERVIEW

Once you've had your person-to-person discussion with a representative of the organization, check out the actual site.

Being there is often the only sure way to get a feel for the organization and the work you'll be doing. Seeing the physical setup of your potential workplace is important. Most of us consciously or unconsciously visualize situations, and later find they are more glamorous in our mind's eye than in reality.

My co-writer once heard about a program that delivered meals to home-bound terminally ill patients and joined without a second thought, but once he showed up to work he discovered that the organization was so poorly run, and the meals so badly prepared, that he didn't blame the recipients who complained that no one, sick or healthy, should have to eat such food.

Try to get an opportunity to observe the operation in the area that interests you before you volunteer. If you like office administration, stop in to see how it's done. If you want to join the education committee, try to attend a meeting as an observer. If you want to do direct service, accompany an experienced volunteer on assignment.

Have conversations with some present members of the organization. This is extremely important. Try especially to contact people assigned to the job you will be likely to have. Bring up with them any questions that your initial interview left unanswered.

Check on the fiscal responsibility of the group. Apart from overall solvency, the main consideration for judging this aspect of a nonprofit organization is the amount of money it actually spends on its programs, as opposed to the costs of administration and fund-raising. It's safe to say that a minimum of 75 percent of money spent should go toward program costs, and many groups and individuals call for an even higher standard, maintaining that 90 percent or more should be spent on programs. Ask both large and small organizations for their annual reports for the last three years. If those publications don't contain information about expenditures, ask how their expense budget breaks down—a standard question which any good organization should be able to answer.

For a third-party report on local groups, contact the Better Business Bureau or the chamber of commerce in your area.

For national organizations, two non-profit watchdog groups can often be helpful:

The National Charities Information Bureau (19 Union Square West, New York, NY 10003; 212-929-6300) provides in-depth reports on more than 300 nonprofit organizations that solicit funds nationwide. Six times a year, it publishes the *Wise Giving Guide,* a summary of its evaluations of all the organizations on which it reports. The guide and up to three individual reports are available free upon written request.

The Philanthropic Advisory Service (PAS) of the Council of Better Business Bureaus (CBBB) (1515 Wilson Boulevard, Arlington, VA 22209; 703-276-0100) collects and distributes information on thousands of non-profit organizations that solicit nationally or that have national or international program services. Every other month, the PAS publishes *Give But Give Wisely,* a concise listing of the most inquired-about charities and whether they meet CBBB standards. The organization also makes available one- to four-page summaries of individual organizations. The guide is available for one dollar, and three reports are available free of charge.

Do your own informal reference checking. Contact other community groups with whom the organization has dealings and ask what they think of this group, what it has accomplished in the community, and how innovative and dynamic it is.

# YOUR OVERALL EVALUATION

A few final questions:

How does the goal of the organization fit with your personal goals, especially your motive for doing service work? It's more than fair to consider whether your interests will be served—for the better the fit, the better the quality of service you'll give.

Sometimes a volunteer and an organization just aren't right for each other. At Outward Bound, we received a letter from an outstanding executive at a Fortune 500 company who was taking early retirement and wanted to become involved. We were thrilled, because the man had so much to offer. But we were a small organization at that time, and we needed help in fund-raising and marketing, rather than in his areas of expertise. Eventually, and sadly, it became clear to both him and the organization that we couldn't make the best use of his considerable talents.

What is the feel of the organization? Do you sense enthusiasm for its stated mission among the people who work there? This is a must. Otherwise, turn elsewhere.

What kind of energy did you sense in the people and in the organization? Is it the kind you like, that you will mesh with?

Do you like the people you met? Do you share the same values?

How did the people you met relate to one another? Are you comfortable with that?

What kind of attitude did you perceive in them about their clients or the program? Do you share a similar attitude?

Based on what you've learned, draw up a brief list of the qualities you think a volunteer for this organization should have. Compare that list with the notes you made in developing your own profile. Are you and this group right for each other?

## MAKING A COMMITMENT

When you feel you want to offer a commitment to a group, it's not appropriate to say you'd like to be on the board or head up the publicity committee as your first assignment, anymore than you'd tell your first boss you want to start overseeing his work. Instead, say, "I want to be involved in this organization. I believe in what you're doing—how can I help?" They'll find something for you to do, and once you've begun, further ways in which you can contribute will develop and more and more responsibility will be offered to you.

Kenneth Dayton, longtime chairman and CEO of Dayton Hudson and a board member of many nonprofit organizations, says: "I think the important thing is for people to decide what they are really interested in, where they can make their contributions, and just let those organizations know [they're available]. If they do that, they'll find that they will be asked [to participate]."

Sometimes an organization will come to you and ask that you become involved, especially if you are a leader in your community or profession. They may want you because of your expertise, your good judgment, your contacts with other influential people. Such overtures give you a wonderful opportunity to discuss fully the work you might do for the organization. Keep an open mind, and don't be so flattered that you fail to examine the place. Your motivation should be strong whether it is you or the organization that makes the first move.

## TIPS FOR NEW VOLUNTEERS

When you begin any endeavor, your enthusiasm is probably very high. Here are a few suggestions for channeling this energy so that you can enter into good works that will lead to as much satisfaction and success as possible.

Be reasonable in making your initial time commitment. It's much better—for you and for the organization—to start with a very realistic and even conservative schedule. You can always lengthen your hours later.

Get to know as many other volunteers as possible. There is no better way to acquire knowledge about the continuity of the group's work and a sense of how programs operate.

Establish some goals for your involvement with the group. Consider how you relate to the aims of the organization now and how you would like to be relating to them in six months or a year. Set objectives for yourself, as you might do in a job, but remain open to new opportunities as the organization changes and as you learn more about it.

Keep your ears and mind open. Leave preconceived ideas behind and discover the spirit of the group. Be conscious of the way in which you begin to contribute. Listen and be sensitive to others' reactions to your ideas. Be positive. People want solution-givers, not problem-starters.

Work in a nondirective way. Nonprofits tend to operate less by top-down, authoritarian methods and more by a consensus approach, channeling of many ideas into a concerted effort to serve the organization's mission. If you insist on a different tack, people may feel they're not being heard, and may lose interest. The best method for leading is to see what consensus is building in the group, and then to move in that direction.

And be ready for anything. Not all organizations are well run. I know of several well-meaning but terribly run programs that have a hard time keeping volunteers around because the directors don't understand the essence of leadership. It's good to listen to everyone, but complete consensus isn't always possible. I've seen organizations stopped cold in their tracks because they weren't able to deal with dissension. As a result, the mission suffered, because too much time was being wasted on internal conflict. So be careful. Be patient. But if it's not for you, then be ready to leave without feeling guilty.

## Taking on More Responsibility

When you first start out, you can expect to attend the meetings of your committee or project group, or begin to fulfill your direct-service assignment. As time goes by and you're found to be an asset, other people will call on you to contribute more. So although you may be involved with mundane sorts of activities at first, as an energetic and willing volunteer you'll eventually take on increasing responsibilities—if you want to.

People and projects gravitate toward the most able and energetic workers. If you're good at what you do, you'll soon be able to serve on various committees; eventually you can afford to be more selective and serve on the committee that holds the most interest for you.

Being appointed or elected to an organization's board is something that you must earn, and your suitability is something that the nominating committee, which recommends people for board membership, will need to evaluate. In order to be recommended, you must earn your stripes, and you can do that by working hard.

## Managing Your Time

Because volunteers handle the time demands of service work in very personal ways, attitudes toward and methods of time management vary considerably.

Some employers who are enthusiastic about outside nonprofit involvement may allow you as much time as you need on the phone or away from the office for direct-service work or appointments. With others you may be able to work out an arrangement to use one hour of the day for your phone work, to take off at particular times for meetings, or to use a couple of hours for a direct-service assignment.

People who don't have a job, or who don't work in an office, face another kind of problem. They're often called repeatedly by those who know their situation and assume they're always available.

If your volunteer work entails a great deal of telephoning, you may want to reach an understanding with your coworkers about when you want to receive calls. You should feel free to be very specific about this, asking people not to call you after 8 P.M., or not before 9 A.M., for instance.

Your associates in the service world will respect your need to organize your life. They're aware of time demands, and know that if they become too great, you may lose your effectiveness, or your work or family life will suffer, and the organization may then lose a valuable member. Balancing the time you really have available with your willingness to serve is going to be one of your top priorities as a volunteer.

It's certainly possible to spend too much time on your volunteer work; then again, even that can have its rewards. My late wife Ellie became very involved in her volunteer work for the British American Chamber of Commerce, so much so that she estimated that it was taking up to 40 percent of her time away from her job at Ward Howell, where she worked as a partner in recruiting. However, it did bring her some tangible rewards, not the least of which were many clients, including her very biggest, Grand Metropolitan. All this led to her becoming one of the top three producers at her company. She was also honored for her volunteer work by Queen Elizabeth, who made her a commander of the British Empire.

## WHAT TO DO IF IT'S NOT WORKING OUT

Even with the best efforts and intentions on your part, it's possible that a particular volunteer assignment or organization may not be to your liking. You and the organization may have misjudged your ability to cope with the assignment. You may have wanted to work with battered children but find that when you do, your emotions overpower your ability to function well. You may realize that the time commitment you made in good faith is in fact unworkable. You may discover that the organization functions in a way that makes you uncomfortable.

If your problem is not with the organization itself but with the assignment or your co-volunteers, try a different job within the same organization. If you're still enthusiastic about the general field but have soured on one organization, try a group that takes a different approach. Or change gears entirely, choosing another field or cause. You'll know more about yourself this time and will have a better chance at making a good match.

If you want to withdraw from an organization, don't just stop showing up. Resign with as much consideration as possible. If it would be helpful, try to give advance notice, as you would in a paid job, or try to complete a project already in progress. One of the most considerate things you can do is find someone to replace you within the organization.

## FINANCIAL AND LEGAL CONSIDERATIONS

There is one other area to consider when you volunteer: giving gifts.

Anyone who makes sizable financial contributions to nonprofit organizations is advised to consult a tax accountant. Still, here are some general guidelines.

In order to take advantage of the deductibility of your contributions, you must itemize deductions on your tax return. The IRS will send you, at no cost, its booklet *Publication 526: Charitable Contributions,* which explains and gives examples of the tax law.

Tax deductions are allowed for contributions to qualified organizations: those that are organized and operated only for charitable, religious, educational, scientific or literacy purposes, or for the prevention of cruelty to children or animals. Certain organizations that foster national or international sports competition are also included. Check with the individual organization about whether your contributions are tax-deductible.

Volunteers can deduct unreimbursed out-of-pocket expenses directly related to the services given to a charitable organization. Contributions that are tax-deductible are:

- Direct monetary gifts
- Nonmonetary contributions of property: for example, clothing, automobiles, office equipment, works of art, securities, real estate (discuss the issue of "fair market value" with your tax consultant)
- Transportation expenses: bus, subway, and cab fares, a portion of automobile mileage, gas and oil, parking fees and tolls
- The expense of maintaining special uniforms
- Telephone bills
- Dues, fees, and assessments
- For tickets to benefits (dinners, concerts, theater events), the difference between the normal price (that is, the fair market value of the meal or admission) and the actual amount paid

Not deductible are:

- The dollar value of your volunteer time or services
- The rental value of property you lend to an organization
- Dependent care expenses (baby-sitting or elder care)
- Gifts to individuals
- Most meals and entertainment, and vacations that may involve some charitable work (discuss these with your tax consultant)

- Automobile repair and maintenance expenses

Keep precise records of the names of organizations to which you donate, as well as descriptions and amounts of contributions. When making monetary contributions, write a check; never give cash. In the case of large gifts, obtain a receipt or statement of donation from the organization.

Once you've made up your mind which organization to join, there is still one more major decision to make, as you'll find out in Part III.

# ROLES TO PLAY

*I know of nothing more despicable and pathetic than a man who devotes all the hours of the waking day to the making of money for money's sake.*

John D. Rockefeller

**O**kay. You've done all your homework, you've talked to three or four different organizations, and now you have picked the one you'd really like to join. Congratulations! You're ready to go.

Almost.

Now it's time to figure out exactly what it is that you'll be doing in your new position.

Just as in your day job, there are many ways to contribute to not-for-profits, at many different levels and in varying functions requiring specialized skills.

These roles fall into three broad categories:

*Direct service,* or one-on-one work with another person, or hands-on support work for the organization.

*Committee work,* or taking on planning, publicity, education, advocacy, development, fund-raising, and other responsibilities, as well as serving on special ad hoc committees or task forces.

*Membership on the board of directors,* whether as a full member, a member of an advisory board, or perhaps as a member of the board's executive committee.

Although these service categories require different skills, they operate together, and without one kind of volunteer work, the others couldn't exist. Furthermore, it's not unlikely that as you volunteer more of your time, you'll move from one of these areas to the others, and enjoy them all equally.

Remember: One of the greatest pleasures of good works is the freedom to decide what you want to do. Don't be bound by your current position or by your sense of your skills. Unlike in a job, where it's practically unheard of to move from the board room to the front lines, in a volunteer position it's not only possible, but can even be fulfilling. In good works, upward and downward mobility are equally possible and equally rewarding.

# DIRECT SERVICE WORK

Direct service comprises hands-on involvement, or the actual implementation of the organization's program. Such work can be a one-time-only project, or part of an ongoing commitment; it can mean working with a small or large group, or with one other person; it can take place in a set location, or can involve moving from place to place.

The category holds tremendous variety. Some of your most valuable skills and talents can be employed in direct-service work.

While many direct-service assignments consist of very basic activity (child care, answering the telephone, cooking, cleaning up, delivery, escorting), such positions—and the services they render—are generally very badly needed by the people or causes served.

Although I've found over the years that all three roles listed above offer a great sense of fulfillment, I personally have never felt better about good works than when I've dealt with another person one on one. And I've found that many direct-service volunteers report a similar profound sense of satisfaction in performing simple tasks in service to others.

In my case, one of the most heartwarming incidents of my life took place in 1997, in the course of my work with the Achilles Track Club, whose mission is to use running as a therapeutic remedy for the disabled. Founded by Dick Traum, the nation's first one-legged marathon runner, the organization now has 140 chapters around the world.

Among its many activities, the club helps its members participate in marathons, with the aid of volunteer helpers. For one recent New York City Marathon I was paired with a former Vietcong soldier whose right leg had been blown off just above the knee by a landmine on the Ho Chi Minh Trail during the Vietnam War. He had become involved in running as therapy through the Achilles Track Club, which has a chapter in Vietnam.

Now he wanted to run the New York City Marathon, so he flew to America with his prosthetic leg to complete the course; I was assigned to help him.

Each disabled runner starts two hours earlier than the rest of the pack, and part of the helpers' job is to shield him or her from the other 28,000 runners as they dash past, as well as helping with whatever need arises during the course of the race.

Together we had a great time, managing to maintain a three- to four-mile-an-hour pace through all five boroughs of New York, and we finished in less than eight hours. All along the way, the crowds cheered my new friend as he struggled and hobbled determinedly along the city streets. People's hearts genuinely go out to these runners, and the goodwill was so overwhelming that several times he stopped to wipe tears from his eyes. Also, twice his leg began to bleed, and we had to have it treated. As for me, I can't remember finishing any race feeling quite as good as after that one.

Direct service doesn't have to be so dramatic, of course. It can encompass anything from sitting with an elderly patient in a nursing home to more complicated, sophisticated, and technical work. It can mean becoming friends with someone in a part of your town you don't know well, or taking care of a neighbor across the street. It can let you indulge a favorite pastime, such as reading aloud, or let you learn a new one, such as a competitive sport. The possibilities are endless.

To describe the scope of direct service, here is a list of services you might perform; it should jog your awareness of your desires as well as your abilities:

## 116 WAYS TO GIVE DIRECT SERVICE

- Serve as an ambulance aide
- Answer the telephone in a telethon
- Assist animal keepers at your local zoo

- Assist a crime victim with sustained personal support
- Lead a bicycling club at a youth center
- Do the bookkeeping for your community center
- Set books in Braille for visually handicapped readers
- Become a buddy to a person with AIDS
- Provide business counsel to a beginning entrepreneur
- Care for a child in a day-care center
- Provide career counseling in a school or community center
- Work with families to stop child abuse
- Teach child care or housekeeping skills at a community center
- Join a cleanup project in a neighborhood, inner-city district, or park
- Offer your clerical skills to a school, arts group, or social-service agency
- Assist in a clinic or blood bank
- Coach a local sports team
- Collect food in a reclamation program
- Comfort children in a hospital
- Donate your computer programming skills to a nonprofit group
- Conduct tours in a museum
- Participate in conflict resolution for community, neighborhood, or family disputes
- Cook for a soup kitchen, shelter, or meals-on-wheels program
- Counsel dropouts or troubled youth

- Become a court-appointed advocate for a child in the foster-care system
- Run a crafts class in an after-school program
- Provide crisis intervention for families in conflict
- Teach daily-living skills to mentally challenged youth and adults
- Deliver meals or food packages to homebound people
- Distribute food to the homeless
- Join an Emergency Medical Service
- Escort hospital and nursing home-patients on outings
- Assist in an exercise program for disabled people
- Provide financial counseling at a community or senior center
- Work with a local rescue group to find homes for stray animals
- Teach first aid or water safety
- Welcome a foreign student into your home
- Become a friendly visitor to a homebound or institutionalized person
- Supervise a game room in a hospital or community center
- Do gardening and landscaping for your community, church, library, or school
- Develop an enrichment program for gifted students
- Take underprivileged children on outings
- Do groundskeeping work for a zoo or botanical garden

- Assist in group-therapy sessions at a youth center or halfway house
- Help a prisoner study for a high-school degree
- Help kids at a dropout center with their homework
- Give classes in home nursing at a community center
- Work in a hospice program for the terminally ill
- Host an inner-city child in your home
- Answer hot line calls
- Help at a Special Olympics event
- Join a program to improve police-community relations
- Staff an information desk at a museum or clinic
- Instruct expectant mothers in childbirth techniques and pre- and postnatal care
- Help integrate an immigrant family into the community
- Interview and test applicants for job training and literacy programs
- Provide job training for the unemployed
- Act as a language interpreter in a hospital
- Maintain the library at a literacy center
- Make clothing for newborn babies in hospitals
- Become a companion at a hospital
- Provide medical or paramedical care at a shelter for battered families
- Become a mentor to a young person

- Provide advice on mortgages, property management, and insurance at a community center
- Conduct nature walks at a botanical garden or park
- Provide nutritional advice at a community center, soup kitchen, or homeless shelter
- Become an ombudsman for a person in a nursing home, monitoring his or her care and practical affairs
- Organize the slide collection at a museum or historical society
- Provide paralegal assistance in a court or public agency
- Assist with patient care in a hospital
- Perform in musical or theatrical presentations in hospitals, prisons, and schools
- Work with animals and people in a pet-assisted therapy program
- Teach photography in an after-school program or at a youth center
- Play with children at a community center
- Prepare beds and meals in a homeless shelter
- Provide pro bono services in law, medicine, management, taxation, or real estate
- Work as a probation aide with a person recently released from jail
- Provide support and reassurance for patients and families in hospital emergency and waiting rooms
- Work in a rape crisis center

- Read textbooks to a blind student
- Read and discuss books and magazine articles in a nursing home
- Be a receptionist at a clinic or hospital
- Collect and separate trash in a recycling center
- Help to rehabilitate housing for the elderly and disabled
- Help relocate families who have lost their homes
- Do remedial tutoring with a college student
- Join a group that rescues animals endangered by pollution
- Run a card party or bingo night at a nursing home
- Become a school volunteer, helping out in a classroom, cafeteria, office, or playground
- Share your experiences at a drug- or alcohol-abuse program
- Socialize with the guests in a homeless shelter
- Sort and distribute mail in a hospital or nursing home
- Spend holidays with institutionalized people
- Sponsor a troop of Girl Scouts, Boy Scouts, or Camp Fire kids
- Organize a stamp, coin, or baseball-card club at a youth or senior-citizen center
- Support the families of the ill, the handicapped, or the mentally challenged
- Test blood pressure in a community health campaign

- Provide tax counseling for senior citizens
- Teach English to a recently arrived immigrant
- Teach job skills to the disabled
- Teach religion classes at your church, synagogue, or mosque
- Teach yoga, aerobics, or modern dance at a community center
- Join a telephone reassurance project, calling elderly or developmentally challenged people once a day
- Be an operator at a teletype deaf hot line
- Organize a theater group in a youth center
- Assist in physical or speech therapy in a hospital or rehabilitation center
- Serve as a trail guide in a park or nature preserve
- Transport elderly or disabled people to and from hospitals and doctors' offices
- Usher at a performance of a dance or theater company
- Become a volunteer firefighter
- Participate in a voter-registration campaign
- Join a walk-a-thon
- Be a weather watcher for the National Weather Service
- Welcome people who've moved into your community
- Donate your word-processing skills or knowledge of computer software to a non-profit group
- Work as a counselor in a summer camp for inner-city children

These ideas are purposefully simple for rapid reading, but most are easy to expand. The list instantly becomes longer, and the number of involvements almost infinite, when you substitute or add words.

As I said, to make a contribution you don't always need the same kind of experience you would if you were applying for a salaried job. For instance, I serve on the board of the Shackleton schools in the Boston area, which you read about earlier. The staff was involved in hiring a new master teacher and I was assisting in the interviews. Most of the applicants had outstanding résumés, but there was one man I remembered more for his character than his experience.

Given how difficult students can sometimes be, at one point I asked him how he dealt with his anger. In response, he told us that he'd recently been in line at a supermarket checkout counter when the young child of the woman in front of him began misbehaving. Finally the exasperated mother slapped the boy across the face, and then continued to abuse him verbally. Our applicant said that his first instinct was to grab the woman. Instead, he waited, calmed down, then followed her to the parking lot, where he handed her one long-stemmed rose. He told her he knew her day hadn't been easy, and that he hoped her life would soon turn a corner.

How could we not hire a man like that? (We did, and he turned out to be a star!)

## COMMITTEE WORK

As they take in new volunteers, many organizations offer beginning assignments in areas other than direct service, such as committee work.

Committees support the efforts of direct-service volunteers, and they also shape ways to set into action the vision and policies created by the board of directors. Joining a committee is basically a matter of showing interest in an organization's work and a willingness to devote the necessary time and effort to implement it.

Once he or she becomes a member of a committee, the volunteer enjoys a wonderful, open-ended opportunity to serve. Enthusiastic and dedicated committee members can often assume leadership positions after a relatively short time. Committee chairmen generally sit on the board of directors, so committee membership is an excellent way to move up within an organization.

In the case of very large nonprofit groups, the structure of the national organization may be reflected on the local level; that is, there may be a national board of directors and national committees and activities, as well as local boards and local committees and activities. Generally, younger (or less experienced) people first become involved in local committees and boards, where there is more hands-on work to be done.

Not every organization will have all the committees mentioned here, and some groups will have ones not covered. But the following discussion should give you a general idea of the playing field.

## THE PLANNING COMMITTEE

This committee is the keeper of the organization's flame. Members of the planning committee develop and plan strategies to implement the group's mission and direct its future. The programs created (for example, direct services, public education, or a fund-raising event) are often the products of close interaction between the planning committee and the board of directors.

The planning committee may be asked to give the board proposals for improved volunteer recruitment, statements of funding needs for the short and long term, or a projected five-year plan.

This kind of work requires the same set of skills you'd bring to a planning operation in the for-profit world: vision, innovation, and sound managerial judgment. Effective members of planning committees should be able to draw up carefully considered goals and objectives; construct useful calendars and budgets; think in both immediate and long-range terms; identify, obtain, and use resources; and put leaders in charge of specific tasks.

When I started as CEO of Outward Bound, one of my first acts was to organize a planning committee. The organization was in a classic turnaround situation: Our programs had some significant safety problems, enrollment was falling, and the national organization was splintering.

Outward Bound had never operated via a national planning meeting, so I decided to call in all the chairmen of the boards of the different Outward Bound schools across the country. We met for four days in Chicago to try to plan the future of the organization.

Once there, we examined all the problem areas and laid out a series of action plans to address them. For instance, part of the planning committee's work was to decide which population group we should try to serve. We had been very successful with the youth program we informally called "Hoods in the Woods" (which, as you might guess, dealt with troubled youth). But we decided that to emphasize this particular program too much would create the wrong public image for the national organization, because we wanted to be associated with leadership skills more than with troubled youth.

Our planning eventually paid off. Within eight years our enrollment grew from 7,500 to 32,000 students, and we instituted a new safety program and a capital campaign, opened urban centers, and entered the field of public-school education with an innovative approach called "Expeditionary Learning."

## THE PUBLICITY COMMITTEE

The publicity committee is in charge of the organization's face to the world, as it interprets the organization's mission and activities for the public. Members' duties range from writing publicity and news releases to editing a newsletter, public speaking, creating public-service ads, organizing mailings, and participating in community fairs. Outreach, such as invitations to prospective clients to join literacy programs, obtain family counseling, or apply for job training, is also part of the publicity effort.

Publicity committee members should be adept at structuring information for interest and readability. They need to be good at understanding the unusual aspects and human-interest angles of organizational news, and to apply basic journalistic principles when presenting facts. In addition, they should understand the print and broadcast media, and how to create material that's easy for them to use. Another essential requirement for publicity committee members, and for all good publicists: an infectious enthusiasm that illuminates the materials and programs they create.

One of my favorite publicists, Cathy Gay, works at the Columbia School of Journalism. She came up with the idea of organizing Columbia breakfasts for noted leaders. Those meals became well known throughout the journalism world. Even though the only preparation they required was obtaining outstanding speakers, some food, and a place to sit, they helped reinforce the school's image as the premier journalism program in the country.

Sometimes publicity also means making the most of the unexpected. One day at Outward Bound, we received a phone call from Camille Cosby, wife of Bill, who wanted to send one of their daughters on an Outward Bound course. The daughter did go, and eventually so did the rest of her siblings. They all enjoyed the trips so much that Bill Cosby joined our board; he also agreed to help us with a major benefit, serving as co-chairman as well as speaker; that event raised a great deal of money. The most unprecedented help he gave us, though, was to write Outward Bound into an episode of the *Cosby Show*, which revolved around Bill's television son going off to an Outward Bound program. This gesture meant millions of people were made aware of our program—people whom we probably never could have otherwise reached.

## THE EDUCATION COMMITTEE

The work of the education committee is related to publicity but goes beyond publicity's domain; rather than spreading the word about the organization itself, the education committee helps familiarize the public with the group's reason for being. In this way, large health organizations might disseminate information about the hazards of smoking, the importance of blood-pressure checkups, and the warning signs of cancer; environmental organizations reach out to inform the public about ecological issues, hoping to raise public consciousness of the issues themselves (and, of course, promote the group along the way).

The two keys to success for the education committee are developing high-quality information presented in an engaging and useful format, and the ability to identify and reach the people who are likely to respond to the information. Some of the fundamental responsibilities of an education committee are:

- Creating articles or news segments for publication or broadcast
- Setting up courses or workshops given by direct-service volunteers
- Organizing lectures by experts for seminars, such as having recovering addicts speak against drug use
- Placing advertisements to increase public awareness about an issue
- Researching issues, conducting public-opinion polls, and publishing the results

One of the most significant responsibilities of the education committee is to obtain pro bono advertising. At Outward Bound, we received over a million and a half dollars a year in donated advertising, including full pages in *Newsweek, Business Week, People, Time,* and many other publications. The advertising agency Ogilvy and Mather was responsible for obtaining this coverage and did the creative work and layout pro bono. How did we cultivate the magazine executive? Each year, we'd invite the publishers and managing editors of major national magazines to participate in a five- or six-day Outward Bound expedition. This personal experience with our mission never failed to produce enthusiastic supporters who in turn gave us the ad space so vital to our organization.

## THE ADVOCACY COMMITTEE

The advocacy committee lobbies for or against certain policies, legislation, and/or behavior. For instance, this committee might encourage businesses to create jobs for youth, the disabled, or ex-offenders. It might speak out against violations of housing-discrimination laws. It could monitor instances of environmental damage or cruelty to animals, or provide court- and police-watching functions. It could promote school breakfast and lunch programs in the inner city.

Advocacy is the principal mission of some nonprofit organizations, such as those that work for the protection of the environment and animals. Along with education, advocacy forms an important part of programs that work for rights and opportunities for those they serve, such as people with diseases and disabilities, or the homeless and hungry.

Perhaps the best-known work in this area is done by the Sierra Club, a strong and articulate voice for environmental protection. Among other issues, it advocates that more land be set aside for parks, and lobbies against various actions that would destroy wildlife areas.

## THE DEVELOPMENT (FUND-RAISING) COMMITTEE

Successful fund-raisers usually work closely with the planning, publicity, education, and advocacy committees. They organize campaigns that clearly express the group's mission and focus on the strongest features of its program. They then focus on motivating potential donors; that is, they pinpoint an individual's, corporation's, or foundation's reasons for becoming involved. Finally, they're careful to inform donors as precisely as possible what the money they've contributed will do for the group.

Nonprofits rely on a large number of fund-raising methods, which are grouped below according to the skills involved in making them work well:

*Marketing skills* come into play in organizing membership drives, door-to-door campaigns, placing canisters on checkout counters, and telephones and direct-mail campaigns.

One of the major reasons Outward Bound did so well in the 1980s was due to the work of John Greene, our marketing vice president, and board member Neil Fox, who had been partly responsible for the popularity of the Vermont Casting Iron Stoves. Neil helped us create a unified image of our program; until then, each of our different schools across the country advertised and marketed itself. He also took us into telemarketing, working out the plan behind an 800 number, so that for the first time we could market our courses via the phone.

*Sound and balanced managerial judgment* must operate within non-profits that charge fees for their services.

*Careful research and persistence* are needed in seeking grants from foundations, corporations, labor unions, and governmental bodies.

*Strong organizational skills* are required for planning and orchestrating the special events that, when successful, provide both funds and visibility. Special events can take the form of galas (concerts, fashion shows, dinners, parties, and balls) and grassroots community events (garage sales, bake sales, raffles, bingo games, carnivals, celebrity bowling or softball, golf tournaments, walkathons, and many more). Special-events organizers need plenty of lead time, many helping hands, and excellent publicity.

When I was working at Outward Bound, we always tried to avoid the sameness associated with the typical fund-raising dinner: the three-course meal, the speech, the heart-warming story, the appeal for money.

To accomplish this, we often went out on a limb—literally. One year we set up a ropes course at the Plaza Hotel. Terrifying the hotel's management, we took over the Terrace Room, dropping ropes down two full stories, which allowed attendees the chance to learn how to rappel. (To guarantee that people were dressed appropriately, the invitation noted that proper attire was black tie and sneakers.)

We also set up balance beams for people to practice walking over water, as well as a Burma bridge, the kind of three-roped narrow walkway most people first saw in the movie *The Bridge Over the River Kwai*.

That evening was an enormous success and became a theme for years to come. But one attempt for a Camp Cook-out Night wasn't. This time we rented a large ballroom space and set up Sterno at every table to heat up roast beef and fish; unfortunately, the Sterno cans didn't generate nearly enough heat to cook the food, and some of us ended up having to send out for pizza. Regardless, we still managed to convey a lesson that all Outward Bounders learn in the woods: You never know when things are going to go wrong, and you have to be flexible enough to adopt an alternative plan.

*The ability to ask for money,* and in the right amount, is key to obtaining either living gifts or bequests from individual large donors.

When you are approaching an individual for a significant donation, it's important to do your homework on the person's background—his or her interests and feelings about the organization—then tailor your approach. For instance, when I was raising money for the Navy Memorial Foundation in Washington, D.C., I wrote to a man I had worked for twenty-five years earlier. He wasn't particularly known for his philanthropy, but I had tied the values on which he'd built his own company to the values that the Navy Memorial Center espoused: self-reliance, self-sacrifice, and courage. Here was a man who had built a great business on these values, and here was an organization seeking to impress young people with these same values.

A week later his assistant called me. She said she couldn't believe it, but she had showed the man the letter and he had nodded thoughtfully; a week later in the mail we received a check for a million dollars.

*Entrepreneurial skills* are needed to create an income-producing business venture and make it successful. Items produced for retail sale may include posters, calendars, T-shirts, mugs, and other memorabilia. Libraries, museums, parks, and other groups often generate income through gift-shop sales of such items.

## THE FINANCE COMMITTEE

This committee's task is crucial. In creating and overseeing both operating and capital-expenditure budgets, the finance committee is responsible for the fiscal health of the organization. With the planning and the development committees, it safeguards the ability of the group to stay alive.

The finance committee sees to it that the organization operates according to its approved budget. It ensures that there is sufficient cash flow to pay bills as they come due, and usually approves any major banking initiatives. The committee reports regularly to the board on the financial health of the organization.

It seems everyone involved in good works has a horror story to tell about their organization's finances. Outward Bound was no different. As I mentioned, when I first arrived, we discovered that our comptroller wasn't doing his job. Now, it's one thing if the comptroller isn't smart about long-term budgeting. But I'm talking about a guy who was taking our bills and shoving them into a drawer.

The most unnerving story I've heard in recent years involved New Era Philanthropy, operating out of Radnor, Pennsylvania. Here what seemed to be a solid foundation turned out to be an old-fashioned Ponzi scheme. New Era's executive director had guaranteed that every dollar received from organizations and individuals would be matched by equal donations from anonymous donors. These donors didn't exist, however, and around $200 million had disappeared. The people deceived by this scheme ranged from Laurence Rockefeller to newscaster Peter Jennings.

Likewise, Bill Aramony did an outstanding job at building United Way, but after many years he began to lose his focus and his moral compass got skewed. During the later years of his tenure as CEO, his salary was out of line with those for leaders of other not-for-profits, and his perks were more like corporate perks; he was also said to be involved in some outside business ventures that were conflicts of interest and therefore unacceptable. Ultimately, he was fired. If the finance committee had been doing its job more carefully, it might have been able to stop this train wreck before it happened. That scandal cost United Way untold millions of dollars and forced it to restaff and rebuild its national organization.

## THE MEMBERSHIP COMMITTEE

For advocacy and cause-related groups, it's essential to have a large and dynamic membership. The membership committee solicits new members and monitors and evaluates the current membership in order to maintain the strength that numbers can bring.

## THE NOMINATING COMMITTEE

Responsible for finding candidates and placing them on the board of directors, the nominating committee plays a key role in determining the quality of an organization's leadership. This committee ensures that the board encompasses the personal resources and professional skills the group needs. Building a board, finding and attracting the strongest members, requires wisdom and hard work. You can greatly influence an organization through your nominations.

For example, in the 1970s I joined the local Congregational Church in New Canaan, Connecticut, and started helping them raise money, which led to my becoming chairman of their stewardship committee. I was then asked to chair the finance committee, which manages the church's budget on such items as building maintenance, and was later asked to become chairman of the board of trustees, which handles the business aspects of the church, as opposed to its spiritual aspect, which are usually overseen by another board.

When my term was drawing to a close, the board asked me to recommend a successor to the nominating committee. I thought this over carefully and realized that the best candidate was a woman who'd been very active in the church. This church had never had a woman as chairman of its board. So although this was a radical departure, I truly believed she'd earned the post through her hard work. Eventually she was accepted, and she did a great job.

## TASK FORCES

Boards of directors occasionally appoint ad hoc committees, often known as task forces, to research facts and opinions in order to recommend solutions to problems.

For example, if a group has no standing planning committee, a task force might be created to develop a training program for volunteers or to decide whether the local youth population would benefit from a counseling program.

# THE BOARD OF DIRECTORS

In most organizations, the nominating committee or executive committee puts forward candidates for the consideration of the current board, whose members then elect the new members to the regular board or to a larger advisory board. The executive committee is made up of a small number of members of the full board.

## THE REGULAR (FULL) BOARD

The board of directors (also known as the board of trustees or the board of governors) makes policy and provides leadership for the nonprofit organization. Among the activities of board members:

- Defining the group's mission and maintaining it as the foremost goal of the organization
- Providing governance to the organization—setting direction, rather than managing or operating
- Setting intermediate goals to support accomplishment of the mission
- Supporting and planning programs to implement the intermediate goals
- Mobilizing resources—money and people—to operate the programs
- Communicating with the people who will serve and support the organization
- Hiring, firing, and advising the executive director and other officers
- Heading or serving on a committee
- Providing for the training of committee members and direct-service volunteers

- Monitoring and evaluating the organization's success in meeting goals and serving the group's stated mission
- Setting the overall style and tone of the organization

Effective boards are composed of a mix of people from varying backgrounds with different kinds of expertise and training.

I think the best board is one that has been consciously shaped to serve the needs of the organization. This sounds obvious, but too often board members are picked for reasons other than their usefulness: because they're friends with other board members, because they're famous, or perhaps because they have promised a great deal of money (and often don't follow through once they're on the board).

Board members should be selected for their ability to do any or all of the following:

- Provide imaginative and sound leadership
- Lend professional expertise to the group's projects
- Communicate the group's mission within their personal and professional circles
- Donate and raise money
- Add credibility and prestige to an organization

In other words, boards are usually open to those with one or more of the three W's: work, wisdom, and wealth. Either you're a worker bee with the energy and desire to get things done, or you're particularly intelligent about the area in which the organization works, or you can contribute a great deal of money.

No board should have only one type of member; it operates best when all three kinds are present. At Outward Bound we were always assessing the board to make sure we kept that balance.

To be a good board member, you must understand the organization's mission and goals, be willing to work, and have a skill to contribute that is related to the traditional aims of the group or to a developing program area.

Bill Baker, the former head of the Westinghouse Broadcasting Company and currently the CEO of WNET in New York City, tells a story about a smart, wealthy man who wanted to join the board of WNET; Baker was delighted with his interest, and agreed to admit him.

When the man arrived, it turned out that his particular business specialties were completely different from those the station needed, and no one could find a way to put the man's talents to work. When he was given a few assignments that required him to function outside of his specialty, he thought he was being asked to work too hard, and he quit.

"Frankly," Baker says, "I think all he wanted to do was have tea with Alistair Cooke."

On the other hand, when Baker needed a lawyer to handle some tough new problems, he called Corey Dunham, the retired general counsel of NBC, who was willing to give his all for the station; he has turned his pro bono work into an almost full-time job.

While each board is different—some are more oriented toward obtaining financial support than others—most nonprofit organizations want their board members at least to help with fund-raising, starting with their own personal contribution. In fact, most groups feel it's vital to have all board members participate in the annual giving campaign.

What board members shouldn't have are aspirations for personal power that will subvert the goals of the organization. Likewise, nominating committees tend to avoid extremely abrasive or confrontational people who would make life difficult in a world that depends on an active and free flow of ideas, and on building eventual consensus.

The size of a board and its meeting schedule depends on the needs of the organization. The board shouldn't be so large as to be unwieldy, but it must be large enough to raise money, generate workable ideas, and provide perspective and problem-solving skills. The board of a medium-size or large organization might consist of between twenty and forty members. Some boards meet quarterly; others meet once a month or eight or nine times a year.

Many boards carry liability insurance to protect their members. In general, the board will meet its legal obligation if members follow—in their individual conduct as board members, in the conduct of the board as a whole, and in shaping the behavior of the organization—the standards of the Philanthropic Advisory Service (PAS) of the Council of Better Business Bureaus (CBBB) and the National Charities Information Bureau (NCIB). The PAS publishes *CBBB Standards for Charitable Solicitations* with sections on public accountability, use of funds, informational materials, fund-raising practices, and the governance of organizations. The NCIB publishes *NCIB Standards in Philanthropy,* a handbook for volunteer board members. (See page 140 for addresses for these organizations.)

I have always felt that it's vital to get board members out of the boardroom and directly into the organization now and then. At Outward Bound we were always trying to take our board out into the field, whether that meant hosting an expedition in the mountains or a rafting trip. These outings for current and prospective board members eventually became very well known and were wonderful sources of new blood for the board. Additionally, the expeditions renewed ongoing board members' enthusiasm for the organization's mission.

For me, the real payback of serving on a board is the intellectual and emotional stimulation you get for making a difference in an organization.

But remember, serving on the board of a not-for-profit isn't necessarily the same as serving on one in the for-profit sector. One friend of mine refers to board work as the punishment you have to endure for being willing to help others. For instance, if you're used to corporate life with its traditional hierarchies, you may be somewhat disoriented by not-for-profits, in which every board member has one vote, instead of the usual scenario in which a senior vice president has more power than a regular vice president. This egalitarianism can make for some tough decision-making, as well as a tendency for each member to think he or she is boss. As a result, things can often get difficult, and making decisions can sometimes take a great deal of time.

## THE EXECUTIVE COMMITTEE

The officers and active members of the full board are often appointed to a committee that works in advance of full board meetings to create agendas and frame issues for discussion; they also act for the full board between board meetings.

The purposes of the executive committee are to channel the energies of the full board by focusing attention on the most important projects, problems, and challenges, and to allow a small group to make decisions in a timely manner when it is impractical to call a full board meeting.

## THE ADVISORY BOARD

An advisory board is generally larger than a regular board. Sometimes honorary, but often functional, it can be used to influence decisions but generally does not make policy.

This board sometimes acts as a training ground for later membership on the full board, and former members of the regular board often remain active as advisory board members. Celebrities and other influential or famous people who are asked to be on a board for purposes of prestige and credibility often participate on the advisory board.

One final note: a ripple effect takes place when you join a board. You're exposed to new people and new circles, and if you do a good job you may well be asked to join other organizations. It's not unusual for people to serve on at least two or more boards at the same time. As of this moment, I serve on ten not-for-profit boards. But I wouldn't recommend that for you. Yet.

Working on this book has allowed me to take an extraordinary journey across the country, talking to scores of women and men about their volunteer experiences and how giving back has impacted their careers in so many unexpected, positive ways.

It's time to think about making that first step so you, too, will have a story to tell some day. Hopefully at least one of the organizations mentioned in the appendix will be the right place for you; but if not, don't worry, for there are thousands more out there.

The one thing all these groups have in common is that they need you. Never have the talents of the women and men in America been more crucial. As government spending at all levels—national, state, and local—has lessened, a much greater burden has fallen on not-for-profits to pick up the slack.

Now couple those very real needs with your own need to make yourself stand out from the crowd in your career, as well to be as well-rounded and respected as you can, and you have a terrific match.

When you start giving back, you'll feel wonderful about what you're doing—that hole inside that prods, "Is that all there is?" will fill up with the satisfaction of good service. And then you will experience the halo effect, and with luck you'll go places in your career that once seemed impossible.

So take that first step. Get involved, as I did so many years ago. Although someone else had to recommend the idea to me, I'm delighted he did, for it made all the difference. Now I'm making that same recommendation to you. Let this book be your mentor, and take the gentle push it's giving you to get involved. I guarantee you, too, will be glad you did.

## Appendix

# A Service Sampler

*You give but little when you give of your possessions. It is when you give of yourself that you truly give.*

Kahlil Gibran

**W**ithin the not-for-profit world, hundreds of thousands of national and local organizations address specific issues and needs, using millions of volunteers along the way. In the following pages you'll find an assortment of such groups—though these represent only a small percentage of all those that exist.

With one or two exceptions, all the organizations listed below are private not-for-profits, but not all directly provide services to people in need; some are volunteer-staffed associations that work on behalf of a group of people or advocate for a cause.

These groups are organized into nine categories:

- Umbrella Groups
- Social Services
- Education
- Culture
- Health
- Environment/Animals
- International Organizations
- Groups of Interest to Children and Youth
- Groups of Interest to Senior Citizens and Retired People

## UMBRELLA GROUPS

Rather than attending to individual needs, **umbrella groups** serve, support, monitor, and represent individual organizations in the private not-for-profit sector. Across the country, more than 2,300 local chapters of United Way and 380 volunteer centers (sometimes called voluntary centers or volunteer bureaus) operate as umbrella groups and clearinghouses. Local chambers of commerce, civic groups, and women's associations are also often excellent sources of information about not-for-profit groups and programs.

**Independent Sector**
1828 L Street NW
Washington, DC 20036
202-223-8100
Web site: http://www.indepsec.org

Independent Sector is a national leadership forum that promotes philanthropy, volunteering, nonprofit initiatives, and citizen action to better serve people and communities. For example, its Give 5 program encourages people to donate five hours per week and/or 5 percent of their income towards volunteering and charitable organizations. Member organizations include some 850 charities, foundations, and religious, social welfare, and other nonprofit organizations and corporate-giving programs.

**InterAction**
American Council for Voluntary International Action
1717 Massachusetts Avenue NW, 8th Floor
Washington, DC 20036
202-667-8236

InterAction aims to enhance the capacities of its membership (private U.S. voluntary organizations) engaged in international humanitarian efforts. Committees focus on development assistance (promoting information-sharing, professional development, and joint action); development education (supporting education on issues relating to Third World development and global interdependence); migration and refugee affairs; resources (especially through its African Emergency Subcommittee); public policy; and private funding. InterAction publishes a collection of profiles on more than one hundred InterAction members, including descriptions of personnel, programs, and financial data.

### National Association for the Advancement of Colored People (NAACP)
4805 Mt. Hope Drive
Baltimore, MD 21215
410-358-8900
Web site: http://www.naacp.org

First created to bring an end to lynchings, today the NAACP is the nation's oldest, largest, and strongest civil-rights organization. Its goal is to achieve equality of rights, eliminate race prejudice, and end racial discrimination. It achieves its ends through nonviolent means, including political pressure, marches, demonstrations, and lobbying. The NAACP maintains a network of more than 2,200 branches in fifty states, Washington, D.C., Japan and Germany, whose officers are volunteers.

### National Charities Information Bureau
19 Union Square West, 6th Floor
New York, NY 10003-3395
212-929-6300
Web site: http://www.give.org

The NCIB provides information about organizations that solicit funds nationally and provides standards for philanthropies. It also provides in-depth reports on nonprofit organizations; its *Wise Giving Guide* summarizes the evaluations of all organizations on which it reports.

**Philanthropic Advisory Service**
Council of Better Business Bureaus
4200 Wilson Boulevard, Suite 800
Arlington, VA 22213
703-276-0133
Web site: http://www.bbb.org/about/pas.html

The Philanthropic Advisory Service (PAS) of the Council of Better Business Bureaus provides information about charities to potential donors to help them make their giving decisions. PAS collects and distributes facts about thousands of nonprofit organizations that solicit nationally or have national or international service programs, and provides one- to four-page summaries about individual organizations. While PAS never recommends one charity over another, it does maintain standards; its bimonthly publication *Give But Give Wisely* offers a concise summary of who does and does not meet CBBB standards.

**United Way of America**
701 North Fairfax Street
Alexandria, VA 22314-2045
703-836-7100
Web site: http://www.unitedway.org

United Way of America is the national membership organization for United Way organizations throughout the United States. United Way itself is a national system of volunteers, contributors, and local charities built on the proven effectiveness of local organizations helping people in their own communities. Its 1,400 independent, locally governed chapters raise funds for community needs, then distribute them to a variety of local organizations, primarily through volunteers. Many chapters serve as clearinghouses to match individuals with volunteer opportunities. United Way of America assists these local United Ways in fund-raising, community problem-solving, distributing funds, and developing and training volunteers. It also works with businesses, governments, and nonprofits to pinpoint and address local issues and build support systems. An international arm was recently added to address human needs in foreign countries.

**U. S. Public Interest Research Group**
218 D Street SE
Washington, DC 20003
202-546-9707
Web site: http://www.igc.apc.org/pirg/uspirg

USPIRG is the national lobbying office and umbrella organization for PIRG chapters in about twenty states—nonprofit, nonpartisan advocacy groups focusing on environmental protection, consumer protection, "student empowerment," and government reform. PIRGs organize at the grassroots level, particularly on college campuses. Volunteers stage petition drives, register voters, canvass door to door on issues, and stage letter-writing campaigns. Recent campaigns have focused on right-to-know, political corruption, product liability, high ATM fees, alternative energy, and many other topics.

## SOCIAL SERVICES

Thousands of national and local groups specialize in providing social services to the needy; they range from programs that give inner-city kids a country vacation to ones that provide disaster relief after a hurricane; others offer assistance and training to the disabled or welcome immigrants to the country. The following comprises only a small share of current programs.

**Soup kitchens** provide meals and **homeless shelters** offer daytime or overnight accommodation. Some have programs to reintegrate the people they serve into independent living through housing placement, literacy and job training, and personal counseling. **Food reclamation programs** collect surplus fresh and packaged food and distribute it to community feeding programs. **Meal delivery programs** take warm or packaged food to the homebound.

**Community centers** and **settlement houses** offer a range of personal and family services, from recreation and education to job training, home-work and mentoring programs for youth, crisis intervention for families, services for seniors, aid for the disabled, community health care, and day care.

Some **crisis centers** and **family support centers** exist specifically to provide respite and shelter for battered wives, abused children, and families with immediate financial emergencies; others offer counseling for drug and alcohol addiction and for youth at risk. Many educate and advocate for the prevention of family abuse.

**Hot lines** of all kinds are channels of help for runaways, people with sexually transmitted diseases, people with AIDS, battered wives, pregnant teenagers, abused children, potential suicides, drug and alcohol abusers, and scores of others. Telephone reassurance programs provide daily contact with the homebound.

**Halfway houses** work with troubled youth, ex-offenders, and others, providing them with the personal, educational, and occupational support that will help them successfully reenter society.

**Senior citizen centers** offer the elderly fellowship and services such as escorting, social outings and nutritional advice, as well as help with health insurance, legal advice, and tax counseling.

Many **civic groups** (such as Kiwanis, Rotary, and Lions Club), **women's clubs,** and **youth groups** offer social-service programs in their local communities, including mentoring for young people, help for the disabled, environmental programs, and assistance to the elderly. Some participate as partners with community social-service agencies.

**Churches, synagogues,** and **mosques** conduct programs of all kinds, both for their own members and for people beyond their congregations: educational programs, personal counseling, fellowship and support groups, soup kitchens and homeless shelters, services for needy children, and programs for senior citizens.

**Public agencies** and **local and state governments** operate many social-service programs, from help for troubled youth and battered children to job training.

For those charged with or convicted of crimes, parolees, and ex-offenders, the **court systems** and **jails** and **prisons** provide programs for support and rehabilitation. Many communities use volunteers to provide personal help for the victims of crime and for children within the foster parents system, among others.

**Police departments** often run programs for local youth. Especially in smaller communities, **fire departments** and **emergency medical services** are frequently staffed by volunteers.

**Political** and **other advocacy groups** (for human and civil rights and environmental and consumer protection, among many other concerns) operate programs with a local, regional, or national focus.

## CHILDREN AND FAMILIES

ASPIRA Association, Inc.
1444 I Street NW

Washington, DC 20005
202-835-3600

Taken from the Spanish word meaning "to aspire," ASPIRA is a national nonprofit organization serving Puerto Rican and other Latino/a youth and their families. Through leadership training and education, it works directly with kids to help them reach their full potential. It also provides training, technical assistance, and public education, and publishes fact sheets on such topics as Hispanic health, education, and violence in both Spanish and English.

**Covenant House**
460 West 41st Street
New York, NY 10036
212-613-0300
Web site: http://www.covenanthouse.org

This Christian mission provides shelter and services to children and youth who are homeless or at risk, especially those who have nowhere else to turn. Covenant House's crisis centers provide street kids with immediate care (food, temporary housing, counseling, medical care), and then help them decide on a course for the future and provide drop-in followup services. Covenant House helps reunite kids with families; it also collaborates with community agencies to improve conditions of families and children; advocates on behalf of suffering youth; offers drug-abuse programs; staffs a crisis hotline; and sponsors Rights of Passage, an eighteen-month transitional program that prepares youths age eighteen to twenty-one for self-sufficient living, matching them with successful adult mentors.

**Family Service America**
11700 West Lake Park Drive
Milwaukee, WI 53224

414-359-1040

Web site: http://www.fsanet.org

FSA is the headquarters organization of a network of some one thousand local agencies throughout the United States and Canada dedicated to helping families. It provides family counseling, family-life education, family advocacy, and other services and programs to assist families with parent-child, marital, mental health, and other problems. For example, its volunteers act as companions, perform crisis intervention, offer transportation to the elderly and disabled, and provide respite care to the ill.

### National Committee for Prevention of Child Abuse

332 South Michigan Avenue, Suite 1600

Chicago, IL 60604-4357

312-663-3520

This organization's goals are to stop child abuse before it occurs, and to create awareness of the problem's causes and effects. Chapters in all fifty states work for prevention through public education, community-based prevention services, research and evaluation, and advocacy.

### National Runaway Switchboard

3080 North Lincoln Avenue

Chicago, IL 60657

800-621-4000

The National Runaway Switchboard is a twenty-four-hour, toll-free hot line providing information and referrals to runaways and other troubled youth and their families. It supplies callers with the names and numbers of shelters and other social services across the country, such as counseling centers, drug treatment facilities, and family-planning services. All services are confidential. The hotline also allows a runaway to relay a personal message to his or her family.

**Spence-Chapin Services to Families and Children**
6 East 94th Street
New York, NY 10128
Web site: http://www.spence-chapin.org

Spence-Chapin provides adoption and adoption-related services and resources, placing infants and young children from the United States and all over the world in permanent homes. It has the largest African-American infant adoption program in the Northeast. Its mission: to promote the image of adoption through counseling and public education; innovative programs allowing birth mothers to choose and work directly with prospective adoptive parents; and a foster-care prevention program, Intensive Families to Children, which provides social services to families in New York City.

## CRIMINAL JUSTICE

**The Fortune Society**
39 West 19th Street
New York, NY 10011
212-206-7070

Based on the idea that the best way to reduce crime is to maximize opportunities for those who have been in trouble in the past, the society works one on one to help ex-offenders and juveniles get back on track. The society provides counseling, tutoring, vocational training, job placement, literacy training, GED preparation, AIDS counseling, and drug and alcohol rehabilitation program referrals. It also offers public education, sending ex-con speakers and panelists to schools and community groups and the media to promote awareness of the prison system and inmate problems before, during, and after incarceration. In addition, the Fortune Society advocates changes in the criminal justice system, including its Alternatives to Incarceration program.

**International Association of Justice Volunteerism**
PO Box 7172
Pueblo West, CO 81007
719-547-3835

Formerly the National Association on Volunteers in Criminal Justice, this organization is committed to improving the juvenile and criminal justice systems through citizen participation. The group sponsors an international forum on volunteers in the criminal justice system; it increases the quality and quantity of voluntary action; improves technical assistance, education, and training of volunteers; establishes guidelines for effective volunteer involvement; develops relationships with other similar organizations; stages seminars and workshops; and acts as an information clearinghouse.

**Mothers Against Drunk Driving**
511 East John Carpenter Freeway, Suite 700
Irving, TX 75062
214-744-6233
Web site: http://www.madd.org

MADD encourages citizen participation in addressing the drunk-driving problem. The group also speaks on behalf of victims to communities, businesses, and educational groups; provides materials for use in medical facilities and health and driver education programs; supports law reform and more stringent laws on alcohol; offers victim assistance, including taking them through the court process; maintains a speakers bureau; and holds workshops.

### DISABILITIES

**Achilles Track Club**
42 West 38th Street, 4th Floor

New York City, NY 10018
212-354-0300

This club is devoted to encouraging disabled people around the world to enjoy the sport of running and to participate in long-distance running alongside the general public. Founded in 1983, it has forty chapters in the United States and another hundred in thirty-six countries around the world, from Mongolia to South Africa. Runners, both experienced and novice, participate on crutches, in wheelchairs, with braces, wearing prostheses, or without any aids at all. Membership is free and includes races, coaching, workouts, team T-shirts, and a newsletter called *The Achilles Heel.*

**The Arc**
500 East Border Street, Suite 300
Arlington, TX 76010
817-261-6003
Web site: http://www.thearc.org

The Arc, formerly the Association for Retarded Citizens, is the country's largest volunteer organization committed to the welfare of developmentally disabled children and adults and their families. The organization works on local, state, and national levels to promote services, research, laws, and public awareness to enhance the lives and independence of developmentally disabled individuals and to reduce the incidence and limit the consequences of its effects. It also provides employment, training, education, and independent-living services to help the disabled maximize their potential through its more than 1,100 affiliate chapters, and it advocates on issues that affect developmentally disabled people and their families, including civil rights, education, self-advocacy, sexuality, and access to justice under criminal law.

**Camp Pacific Heartland**
3663 Wilshire Boulevard
Los Angeles, CA 90010

213-464-1235
Web site: http://www.camppacificheartland.org

This nonprofit organization, founded by Hollywood producer David Gale, arranges for children and adolescents who are infected with or affected by AIDS/HIV to attend a weeklong camp in Malibu. While enjoying the outdoors and carefree activities, campers can make friends and talk with others who share their situation; they receive complete medical care. Camp Pacific Heartland also trains and places former campers and camp staff as speakers at schools, to talk about AIDS and raise funds for the camp's programs.

**Goodwill Industries International**
9200 Wisconsin Avenue
Bethesda, MD 20814
301-530-6500
Web site: http://www.goodwill.org

Goodwill agencies provide job training, evaluation, counseling, placement, and other services to people with disabilities, special needs, and other barriers to employment. Goodwill Stores, which collect, process, and sell donated materials such as clothing and appliances, furnish the funds to sustain Goodwill's work and provide jobs to the people it helps.

**Recording for the Blind (RFB)**
20 Roszel Road
Princeton, NJ 08540
609-452-0606
Web site: http://www.rfbd.org

Recording for the Blind loans recorded educational books free to the blind and reading-disabled. It currently maintains almost five thousand volumes (all recorded by volunteers); new titles are added each year. Recording for the Blind also offers library services, computerized books, and other educational materials, operating more than thirty recording studios across the country. Volunteers must have completed at least two years of college and donate two hours of their time per week. Specialists in computers, law, medicine, and the sciences are especially needed.

**Special Olympics**
1325 G Street NW, Suite 500
Washington, DC 20005
202-628-3630
Web site: http://www.specialolympics.org

Special Olympics was created by the Joseph P. Kennedy, Jr. Foundation to promote physical fitness, sports training, and athletic competition among developmentally disabled kids and adults. It seeks to contribute to the physical, social, and psychological development of the developmentally disabled by staging local, area, and chapter games in 140 countries. The group runs competitions in track and field, swimming, gymnastics, bowling, ice skating, basketball, and many other sports. Every four years the organization sponsors the Special Olympics World Summer and World Winter Games. It also maintains a speakers' bureau, collects statistics, and sponsors research.

### DISASTER RELIEF

**American Red Cross**
430 17th Street NW
Washington, DC 20006-2401
202-737-8300
Web site: http://www.redcross.org

The American Red Cross provides relief to victims of disasters and helps people prevent, prepare for, and respond to emergencies. A heavily volunteer organization, the Red Cross is one of the largest humanitarian organizations in the United States. Activities include disaster planning, preparedness education, and relief; health and safety services, including training in CPR, first aid, water safety, and HIV/AIDS; direct health services such as first aid and health screenings; blood drives, which provide blood products and tissue services, supplying about half the nation's blood supply; emergency communications and assistance to members of the armed forces and their families; international disaster relief and preparedness training; and humanitarian assistance abroad in more than 170 nations.

## IMMIGRANTS

**The International Center in New York**
50 West 23rd Street, 7th Floor
New York, NY 10010
212-255-9555
Web site: http://www.mindspring.com/~icny

The International Center offers a variety of programs to help recently arrived foreigners adjust to American life. It aids students, foreign emissaries and trainees, refugees, and legal immigrants. The center also provide English lessons, arranges appointments, counsels on personal problems, provides job and housing assistance, arranges visits to local homes, and stages orientation programs and sightseeing tours.

## POVERTY AND URBAN RELIEF

**Association of Community Organizations for Reform Now (ACORN)**
739 8th Street SE
Washington, DC 20003

202-547-2500
Web site: http://www.acorn.org/community/

ACORN organizes people in low- and moderate-income communities and helps empower them to address community needs, often going door to door to recruit new members. Some of its major campaigns mobilize around projects such as organizing unions; starting community media such as local cable TV and radio stations; and revitalizing deteriorating neighborhoods by buying and rehabilitating abandoned buildings. In the past, ACORN has helped secure bank loans for low-income housing; improved neighborhood schools; registered voters; stopped or helped clean up toxic plants and dumps in poor neighborhoods; and boosted neighborhood safety.

**Habitat For Humanity**
11 Habitat Street
Americus, GA 31709-3498
912-924-6935
Web site: http://www.habitat.org

Popularized by former President Jimmy Carter, this Christian housing ministry aims to eliminate substandard housing in the world. Working with families unable to afford a commercial home loan, the group builds low-cost housing; recipients live in the house and pay back the loan with no interest. Teams of volunteers help with construction at local project sites and work internationally in more than 1200 projects in developing countries. Recent projects have consulted with environmental groups to build "green" homes that utilize sustainably produced construction materials and energy-efficient designs. All funding and materials are donated.

**National Coalition for the Homeless**
1612 K Street NW, Suite 1004

Washington, DC 20006
202-775-1322
Web site: http://nch.ari.net

The National Coalition for the Homeless is an advocacy network committed to ending homelessness through public education, policy advocacy, grass-roots organizing, and technical assistance. Besides connecting homeless people with transitional homes, apartments, and emergency shelters, the coalition sponsors many educational and organizing projects, special campaigns, and annual events. For example, the Education Rights Project works to support the right of homeless children to attend school; the "You Don't Need a Home to Vote" campaign registers thousands of homeless people to vote and protects and promotes their right to do so. It also helps street newspapers produced and sold by homeless people and sponsors collections of poetry and art created by the homeless, among other activities.

**The National Urban League**
500 East 62nd Street
New York, NY 10021
212-310-9000
Web site: http://www.nul.org

The National Urban League is a nonpartisan interracial community-service organization working to ensure equal opportunities in all sectors of societies for African-Americans and other members of minority groups. The League works through direct service to assist minority-group members with job placement and training, housing, and health care; performs research on social and economic issues; provides information for use in forming public policy both nationally and locally; advocates for African-Americans and other minorities and the poor; and builds bridges between black and white America.

**Volunteers in Service to America (VISTA)**
1100 Vermont Avenue NW, Suite 8100
Washington, DC 20525
202-606-4845
Web site: http://www.americorps.org/ac_vista.html

VISTA is a full-time, year-long volunteer-service program in the United States and its territories, run by AmeriCorps, an independent government agency. Men and women of all ages and backgrounds commit themselves to improving the self-sufficiency of low-income people and enhancing the conditions of their lives. Volunteers live and work among the poor, serving in urban and rural areas and on Indian reservations, where they share their skills and experience. VISTA services include education and literacy programs, employment training, food distribution, shelter for the homeless, and drug-abuse treatment. It also works with runaway youth, assists senior citizens, and helps with neighborhood revitalization.

**SHUT-INS**

**The Holiday Project**
2029 Vista Lane
Petaluma, CA 94954
707-763-5621

The Holiday Project began in 1971, when eight people in San Francisco joined together on Christmas day to visit patients and share a holiday dinner in a local hospital. Over the years, the project has grown to include Chanukah as well as Christmas, in addition to visits to prisons, nursing homes, psychiatric facilities, shelters for victims of domestic violence, juvenile detention homes, orphanages, and facilities for the developmentally and physically disabled. Besides visiting, volunteers can help organize visits, make gifts, and provide entertainment.

## WOMEN'S ISSUES

### The Association of Junior Leagues International, Inc.
660 First Avenue
New York, NY 10016-3241
212-683-1515

The Association of Junior Leagues International, Inc., is an organization of women committed to promoting volunteerism, developing the potential of women, and improving their communities through the effective action and leadership of trained volunteers. The organization develops, supports, and runs activities in the areas of domestic violence assistance, literacy, mentoring and school readiness, transitional service for the homeless, well-child and preventive health care for children, and family support programs. There are 292 chapters in the United States, Canada, Mexico, and England. Each Junior League is independently incorporated in its community and responsible for developing and implementing its program based on community needs.

### League of Women Voters Education Fund
1730 M Street NW
Washington, DC 20036
202-429-1965
Web site: http://www.plannedparenthood.org

The educational arm of the League of Women Voters aims to increase public understanding of public-policy issues, promote voting, and encourage more active and effective citizen involvement in government and the democratic process. The league provides a variety of services, including research, education, litigation, and publications; it also stages conferences on current public-policy issues including voting, nuclear waste, social welfare, international relations, and health care.

**Planned Parenthood Federation of America**
810 Seventh Avenue
New York, NY 10019
212-541-7800
Web site: http://www.plannedparenthood.org

Planned Parenthood Federation and its 169 affiliates and 900 health-care centers and clinics aim to make voluntary contraception, abortion, sterilization, and fertility services available to all. The organization provides medical services, counseling, education on sexuality and reproduction, counseling, and advocacy for reproductive rights to women and men; it produces education programs, materials, and curricula, and works on issues such as teen pregnancy prevention, AIDS education, and international family planning.

**Women in Community Service**
1900 North Beauregard Street
Alexandria, VA 22311
703-671-0500

WICS is an independent coalition of five major national women's service organizations (American GI Forum Women, Church Women United, National Council of Catholic Women, National Council of Jewish Women, and the National Council of Negro Women). The organization works in communities to improve the quality of life for women and youth in poverty, combining resources to coordinate efforts. WICS provides educational opportunities, vocational training, employment, and dependent care; it offers Job Corps referral and support, identifies job opportunities, and provides training and services before, during, and after Job Corps training.

## OTHER

### AmeriCorps
c/o Corporation for National Service
1201 New York Avenue NW
Washington, DC 20525
202-606-5000
Web site: http://www.americorps.org

A relatively new national service program, AmeriCorps allows people of all ages and backgrounds to earn dollars to pay for education in exchange for a year of community service. AmeriCorps meets community needs around the country with projects in four areas: education, public safety, human services, and the environment. Activities range from renovating housing to child immunization to neighborhood policing, tutoring teens, helping crime victims, visiting shut-ins, and restoring coastlines. AmeriCorps also helps involve all sectors of the communities it serves in its activities, from planning through implementation.

### Christmas in April USA
1536 16th Street NW
Washington, DC 20036
202-483-9083
Web site: http://www.christmasinapril.org

This volunteer-based program rehabilitates the homes of low-income, elderly, and/or disabled homeowners at no cost to them, so that they may continue to live safely and independently. Working in partnership with the community, Christmas in April recruits and organizes skilled and unskilled volunteers to paint, clean, weatherize, perform carpentry, fix plumbing, and do electrical work using supplies that are donated or purchased by the program. Each April, Christmas in April programs across the country participate in a National Rebuilding Day to rehabilitate homes and nonprofit facilities. Each of its 185 local chapters is self-managed (with help available from the national office) and sets its own goals.

**Veritas**
912 Amsterdam Avenue
New York, NY 10025
212-865-9182

Veritas, founded in 1971 and run by Jim Little, is a residential treatment facility for men and women with serious addictions, along with their families and children. Multi–award winning, it offers several programs, including one for mothers and infants, full vocational services, housing for those who have completed treatment but can't afford to rent a place in New York City, and an outpatient program for children and families of residents. Volunteers supply three major services for Veritas: They provide training for residents trying to obtain a general equivalency diploma, offer job mentoring, and are also the core of a business advisory council which advises graduating residents trying to find work.

**REGIONAL**

**Community Impact**
3921 East Bayshore Road
Palo Alto, CA 94303
650-965-0242
Web site: http://www.communityimpact.org

This nonprofit volunteer organization in the San Francisco Bay area is dedicated to making community service easy and fun by creating flexible and unique volunteer activities. In cooperation with local nonprofits, Community Impact organizes one-day projects each week. There are projects in four areas: facilities (such as building playgrounds); people (such as tutoring homeless children); environment (such as restoring trails); and organizations (such as sorting groceries for food banks). Each project is designed and coordinated by volunteer project teams.

**Focus: Hope**
1355 Oakman Boulevard
Detroit, MI 48238
313-494-4400
Web site: http://www.focushope.edu

Operating in Detroit and its suburbs, this interracial movement of volunteers devises and implements creative and practical programs to help overcome racism, poverty, and injustice and build a harmonious metropolitan community. Focus: Hope has started many initiatives to serve low-income minority communities, including several for-profit companies that provide career opportunities in the neighborhood. These include the Food Prescription Program, which provides supplemental food to mothers and children; a Center for Children, which offers day care and preschool education; a Center for Advanced Technologies, a manufacturing engineering program; the Machinist Training Institute, a technical education and training program; Fast Track, which prepares young adults for training at the MTI and CAT; and programs for seniors.

**Fresh Air Fund**
1040 Avenue of the Americas
New York, NY 10018
212-221-0900
800-367-0003 (to host)
Web site: http://www.freshair.org

Since 1877, the Fresh Air Fund has provided free summer vacations (including transportation) in the country or suburbs to almost two million disadvantaged inner-city children from the five boroughs of New York. Fresh Air Fund kids come from low- income families, most on public assistance, who are registered with various social-service and community organizations. Through the Friendly Town program, boys and girls ages six to eighteen visit volunteer host families in thirteen states from Virginia to Maine and Canada, or one of the Fund's five camps in Fishkill, New York, for one or two weeks. Many kids are invited back to join the same families year after year. There is also a Career Awareness Program for kids ages twelve to fifteen that helps New York City youngsters understand and prepare for the world of work.

**Human Service Alliance**
3983 Old Greensboro Road
Winston-Salem, NC 27101
910-761-8745
Web site: http://www.hsa.org/service

The nonprofit Human Service Alliance has attracted national and international attention for its unique way of offering service (see page 58). Staffed and run 100 percent by volunteers, HSA provides all services completely free and directs all donations directly to support them. HSA works in four areas: It provides twenty-four-hour residential care for terminally ill people, cares for severely disabled children so their parents can have time off, diagnoses and treats people with chronic pain and teaches them wellness skills, and provides a mediation and dispute-resolution service. The organization also trains those interested in learning to set up and run all-volunteer organizations.

**New York Cares**
116 East 16th Street, 6th Floor
New York, NY 10003
212-228-5000
Web site: http://www.ny.cares.org

New York Cares runs hundreds of hands-on, direct volunteer-service projects in all five New York boroughs, planned in partnership with schools, social and human-service agencies and environmental organizations. Working in teams, volunteers tutor children, feed the hungry, assist people with AIDS, plant gardens, visit the elderly, paint and renovate community centers, and more. Projects take place on weekends and weekdays before or after working hours, making service easier for participants. New York Cares also helps civic-minded companies organize their own projects. Annual New York Cares events include a Coat Drive to collect used coats for homeless people and others, and a Secret Santa program that fulfills wishes and gives gifts to needy children.

## EDUCATION

**Elementary** and **secondary public** and **private schools** offer numerous programs, many run by volunteers, that go beyond their basic curricula, including special classes in nonacademic subjects, remedial tutoring, work with gifted students, after-school activities and clubs, sports programs, and day care. Other volunteers work as street-crossing guards, vocational and personal counselors, and aides on playgrounds and in classrooms, cafeterias, and libraries. Public schools are directed by boards of education and private schools by voluntary boards of directors. Parent-teacher organizations often form an important channel for community contributions to schools. For private schools, fund-raising programs are critical.

**Colleges** and **universities** rely on the participation of able and interested people to serve as directors and advisers. Institutions of higher education offer many supplemental educational programs, including remedial tutoring, and special help for foreign and disabled students. Alumni form the core of volunteer groups at many schools.

In addition to the schools themselves, many groups address educational issues and problems, offering a variety of solutions.

**Adopt-A-School (Los Angeles program)**
Los Angeles Unified School District
450 North Grand Avenue, Room H-237
Los Angeles, CA 90012
213-625-6989

Hundreds of Los Angeles–area schools have been "adopted" by local businesses in this program wherein companies make their resources available to help enrich a school's educational programs; because each school has a different set of needs and companies have different resources, each adoption is unique. Programs have provided tutoring, mini-course lectures, hobby sharing, career counseling and awareness, club sponsorship, parent workshops, teacher workshops, and student employment.

**The Great Books Foundation**
35 East Wacker Drive, Suite 2300
Chicago, IL 60601-2298
312-332-5870
Web site: http://www.greatbooks.org

The Great Books Foundation provides people of all ages with the opportunity to read, discuss, and learn from great works of literature. It also publishes paperback books of readings for discussion and administers training courses that prepare volunteers, teachers, and librarians to conduct junior and adult Great Books groups. Adult groups meet in private homes, libraries, offices, and churches and discuss the ideas of great thinkers and writers; a junior group is available for students in kindergarten through twelfth grade.

**I Have a Dream Foundation**
330 Seventh Avenue, 20th floor
New York, NY 10001
212-293-5480
Web site: http://www.ihad.org

In 1981, multimillionaire businessman Eugene Lang offered to pay for the college educations of a class of inner-city sixth graders if they finished high school; the project was hugely successful, as 90 percent of them did. In 1986, Lang started the I Have a Dream Foundation to support other such projects, which "adopt" classes of poor youth in schools and public housing, and then mentor them for as many as ten to twelve years. During this time, volunteer leaders provide academic and moral support and sponsor cultural and recreational activities for every member of the class. The goal: to help sponsored students, called dreamers, to graduate from high school and then to complete college or find a good job. The IHAD foundation also acts as a clearinghouse for ideas and programs for IHAD projects, conducts seminars and training programs for sponsors and project coordinators, and provides tuition assistance to students.

**Literacy Volunteers Of America**
5795 Waterside Parkway
Syracuse, NY 13214
315-445-8000
Web site: http://www.cgim.com/lva

This organization combats the problem of adult illiteracy in America through hundreds of local groups that train and assist individuals and organizations to tutor adults in basic reading and English as a second language. Volunteer tutors complete a course (provided by Literacy Volunteers) in special adult-literacy education techniques, after which each person is matched with a learner whose personal and professional goals determine the course of study. Literacy Volunteers also provides training materials and services nationwide to volunteer literacy programs, and compiles literacy statistics.

**National Association of Partners in Education, Inc. (NAPE)**
901 North Pitt Street, Suite 320
Alexandria, VA 22314
703-836-4880
Web site: http://www.napehq.org

NAPE is the only national membership organization devoted solely to providing leadership to develop partnerships that improve the academic and personal growth of America's youth and help kids acquire the citizenship and workforce skills they need for the future. In these partnerships, schools or school districts collaborate with one or more community organizations and businesses—companies, universities, the media, health care organizations, labor groups, foundations, and government agencies, among others—to develop and implement integrated support services to help every student succeed.

**The National PTA (National Congress of Parents and Teachers)**
330 North Wabash Avenue, Suite 2100

Chicago, IL 60611-3690
312-670-6782
Web site: http://www.pta.org

A nonprofit volunteer association with chapters in every state, the National PTA advocates for the interests of children and teenagers and strives to unite the forces of home, school, and community on kids' behalf. The organization works for legislation benefiting children and monitors laws related to youth, and offers programs addressing drug and alcohol abuse prevention, HIV/AIDS education, single parenthood, discipline, and latchkey children, and sponsors parent-education meetings.

**Outward Bound**
Route 90, R2 Box 280
Garrison, NY 10524
914-424-4000
Web site: http://www.outwardbound.org

Outward Bound, the largest and oldest outdoor-education program in the country, operates five wilderness schools and ten urban centers designed to help adults and young people develop leadership skills, self-esteem, a sense of service, and sensitivity to the environment by confronting a series of increasingly difficult physical and mental tasks. Each school offers courses lasting anywhere from four to ninety days that cover physical conditioning, technical training, expeditions, environmental conservation, and community service. Outward Bound also teaches technical skills such as mountaineering, camping, rock climbing, rafting, sailing, emergency medical aid, and search and rescue; it offers programs on substance abuse and mental health, as well as professional-development courses for managers at all levels. Outward Bound also trains a variety of community service volunteers.

**Reading Is Fundamental (RIF)**
600 Maryland Avenue SW, Suite 500

Washington, DC 20024
202-287-3220
Web site: http://www.si.edu/rif

Reading Is Fundamental (RIF) is a national organization that sponsors grass-roots reading-motivation projects for millions of children. Through imaginative activities that bring books to life, the project seeks to make reading meaningful and fun for students from pre-kindergarten to grade twelve; to help parents encourage reading at home; and to allow kids to choose and own free books that interest them.

## CULTURE

**Libraries** are often staffed partially or totally by volunteers. While some are supported by government money, many owe their existence to the efforts of fund-raisers and the creativity of volunteer trustees. Some publicly and privately funded libraries use volunteers in on-site programs in which children hear books read aloud, young people and adults get instruction in reading and writing, and the visually disabled are assisted with special materials. Others send volunteers out in visitation programs to hospitals and nursing homes, where books are read aloud and discussions held.

**Museums** and **historical societies** train volunteer docents (people who conduct group tours through galleries or exhibits) to guide the public to a fuller appreciation of their holdings. Many integrate volunteers into their newsletter staffs and other educational activities, as well as their labeling and catalogue work.

**Dance, theater, opera,** and **musical organizations** are often supported by actively involved boards of directors and fund-raisers. Financial and legal professionals sometimes contribute their expertise pro bono. These cultural groups call on other volunteers to assist with functions from ticket-taking and ushering to constructing scenery, administration, advertising and promotion, and office work.

**Public television** and **radio stations** are supported by funds raised from corporations, foundations, and individuals, and by the efforts of volunteers who donate their professional expertise in publicity and programming, assist in administration, and perform clerical tasks.

**Community** and **neighborhood newspapers** are often designed, written, and produced on a voluntary, nonprofit basis.

American Association of Museums
1575 Eye Street NW, Suite 400
Washington, DC 20005
202-289-1818
Web site: http://www.aam-us.org

The American Association of Museums advances the welfare of the nation's museums. In addition to political activism on behalf of cultural and educational organizations, the association accredits museums and places museum professionals in jobs. Member museums include art, history, and science museums, art associations and centers, historical societies, planetariums, zoos, and botanical gardens. Volunteer opportunities abound within such institutions; some smaller museums are staffed solely by volunteers, and even the largest urban institutions rely heavily on volunteers as guides, cataloguers, fund-raisers, trustees, and participants in multilingual programs, assistants for traveling exhibits, junior and senior citizen guides, and so on.

### American Museum of Natural History
Central Park West at 79th Street
New York, NY 10024
212-769-5000
Web site: http://www.amnh.org

This museum, long beloved by generations of schoolchildren for its dinosaur skeletons and astronomy shows, maintains scores of permanent and temporary exhibits, along with educational and research programs focusing on natural sciences (especially evolutionary biology, zoology, and mineralogy) and anthropology. The museum also runs the Hayden Planetarium and publishes *Natural History* magazine. It uses an unusually high percentage of volunteers, who work both with the public and in various internal departments.

### American Poetry and Literacy Project
1058 Thomas Jefferson Street NW
Washington, DC 20007
202-338-1109

The goal of the American Poetry and Literacy Project (APL) is to encourage literacy by distributing some 20,000 free volumes of poetry. Mostly through volunteers, APL supplies poetry to schools, libraries, hospitals, homeless shelters, jury waiting rooms, subway stations, train stations, airports, hotels, and literacy programs across the country. Through donations, books are bought directly from publishers; the project's latest effort is distributing collections of African-American poetry. Volunteers also help organize poetry readings, coordinate fund-raising activities, and select and place poetry in the Yellow Pages.

**American Symphony Orchestra League**
1156 15th Street NW, Suite 800
Washington, DC 20005
202-628-0099

The American Symphony Orchestra League is a national service and educational organization for the nation's symphony orchestras. It works on behalf of everyone involved, from musicians and conductors to management and trustees. The league also has a Volunteer Council that develops services for orchestra volunteers. It performs research on various facets of symphony orchestra operations and development; provides consulting services for orchestras and related boards; holds workshops and seminars for administrators, players, volunteers, and management; and collects data on symphony orchestras. Volunteers can participate in board leadership roles, fund-raising projects, ticket sales campaigns, educational projects, and community relations.

**Arts & Business Council**
25 West 45th Street, Suite 707
New York, NY 10036
212-819-9287
Web site: http://www.artsandbusiness.org

The Arts & Business Council's "Business Volunteers for the Arts" program facilitates partnerships between the business and arts communities in

New York and some twenty-eight major metropolitan areas, including Chicago and Houston. It trains corporate executives as volunteer arts-management consultants, then places them with nonprofit arts organizations in fields such as music, dance, art, and arts education, most of which are small and cannot afford their own staffs. Volunteers may consult in fields such as communications, graphic design, financial planning, data processing, information systems, and marketing, among others, and must commit to one year of service and complete a training course.

**Big Apple Circus**
35 West 35th Street
New York, NY 10001
212-268-2500

This nonprofit performing-arts organization presents some of the finest classical circus arts in America, complete with clowns and prancing horses. The circus' intimate one-ring show is seen by more than half a million people in New York City and throughout the Northeast each year. Part of the Big Apple Circus's mission is to provide outreach services in the communities where it performs; its Clown Care Unit, for example, sends clowns into hospital pediatric wards, and its Ticket Fund offers free and subsidized tickets to community groups. Volunteers serve as ambassadors to the public, working on site during performance season; among other tasks, they assist in the development and marketing departments, answer audience questions, and pass out red clown noses to members (financial supporters); they also help staff special events.

**Metropolitan Museum of Art**
1000 Fifth Avenue
New York, NY 10028
212-879-5500
Web site: http://www.metmuseum.org

"The Met" is one of the largest fine art museums in the world. Its collections include more than two million works of art, spanning more than five thousand years of world culture from prehistory to the present—several hundred thousand of which are on view at any given time. Some of the more famous of its departments include the Arms and Armor collection, Egyptian Art, the American Wing, European Paintings, Musical Instruments, and the tapestries at the Cloisters, along with special exhibitions. A new program, the Apollo Circle, provides museum-related education and social activities especially for patrons ages twenty-one through thirty-nine. The museum has a very large volunteer staff working in its libraries, offices, and curatorial departments and serving as tour guides to students, seniors, and disabled visitors. Training programs for volunteers require a substantial effort and commitment; the museum in turn offers lectures throughout the year on various aspects of its collections and exhibits.

**National Public Radio**
635 Massachusetts Avenue NW
Washington, DC 20004
202-414-2000
Web site: http://www.npr.org

NPR is a private nonprofit organization with hundreds of member stations. It is the only nationwide, interconnected public radio system in the United States, and broadcasts in-depth news, cultural programs, and other programs live via satellite, including the highly popular show "All Things Considered." Besides programming, NPR provides member stations with support services. Volunteers are the backbone of its audience services unit; they respond to phone calls and letters, research information, and fulfill cassette orders; as well, individual member stations often use volunteers to supplement their staffs.

**National Trust for Historic Preservation**
1785 Massachusetts Avenue NW

Washington, DC 20036
202-673-4000
Web site: http://www.nthp.org

The National Trust for Historic Preservation encourages public participation in the preservation of sites, buildings, and objects significant in American history and culture. It fights to save our historic and architectural heritage from destruction, and to retain and revitalize the special historic quality of America's Main Streets. The organization also helps protect and restore districts, older neighborhoods, homes, and urban waterfronts; maintains historic properties; offers low-interest loans and grants and legal advice; and serves as a clearinghouse for information about historic buildings.

**Oregon Shakespeare Festival**
15 South Pioneer Street
PO Box 158
Ashland, OR 97520
503-482-2111
Web site: http://www.orshakes.org

Attracting hundreds of thousands of visitors each year, the Oregon Shakespeare Festival presents plays by both classic and modern dramatists—including, of course, Shakespeare—from February through October. Volunteers are involved in every aspect of the operation, including working at a garden club and a festival exhibit center; serving as hosts, board members, endowment trustees, or on a welcome team for new company members; participating in the Tudor Guild, which provides financial assistance to company members and studies Shakespearean literature; and acting as relief volunteers, who help during "overload" times in the costume shop or the box office.

**Volunteer Lawyers for the Arts**
1 East 53rd Street, 6th Floor

New York, NY 10022
212-319-2787
Web site: http://www2.ultra.net/~barweb/vla/index.htm

Volunteer Lawyers for the Arts provides the arts community with free legal assistance and education. Artists and arts organizations that have arts-related legal problems and cannot afford private counsel are eligible for VLA's services. VLA has some thirty chapters around the country and works with all creative fields, including literature, dance, theater, music, film, and the visual arts. Attorneys donate counseling and representation on matters such as libel, copyright, patents and trademarks, contracts, insurance, labor relations, housing, loft and performance space, nonprofit incorporation, and tax exemption. In New York, an "Arts Legacy" project helps creative people with AIDS plan for the future management of their estates.

**WNET**
356 West 58th Street
New York, NY 10019
212-560-2000
Web site: http://www.wnet.org

Thirteen/WNET, the New York City area's PBS station, is a nationally recognized innovator in television programming and educational products and services that move beyond the screen. But it's perhaps best known for broadcasting such perennial favorites as "Masterpiece Theater," "Nature," "Great Performances," "Nova," "The NewsHour with Jim Lehrer," and countless specials, news, documentaries, children's programs and educational shows. As well, WNET operates a World Wide Web "station," which offers programs based on WNET's on-air shows, and Learning Link, one of the oldest and largest educational on-line networks; runs a national teacher-training institute that trains teachers to use TV as an interactive instructional tool; and has telephone help lines offering viewer information on important issues. The station forms partnerships with New York–area organizations for projects such as Act Against Violence Day. Among other things, volunteers are needed to answer phones for its frequent fund-raising pledge drives.

**Young Audiences (YA)**
115 East 92nd Street
New York, NY 10128
212-831-8110
Web site: http://www.youngaudiences.org

Young Audiences is the nation's largest performing-arts education organization. Each year, it selects and trains professionals to stage specially designed participatory music, dance, and theater programs for children in kindergarten through grade twelve during school hours. The goal is to help kids appreciate the arts and develop their own creative skills. YA chapters serve big cities and small towns and are increasingly branching out into libraries, museums, parks, and other public places to present community arts programs involving both children *and* adults. Its Advisory Artists, who have included the likes of Wynton Marsalis, sometimes offer master classes and other special events.

**Young Musicians Foundation**
195 South Beverly Drive, Suite 414
Beverly Hills, CA 90212
310-859-7668

This classical music foundation maintains eleven different programs to support and develop talented young musicians. For example, it runs a professional training orchestra for youth up to age twenty-five; auditions kids ages eight through twelve nationwide, then brings them to music camp, culminating in concerts aired on the Disney Channel; sponsors a chamber-music program for instrumentalists up to age seventeen and vocalists up to age twenty-five; performs educational outreach; and places music teachers who work for free in public schools (teachers are graduate-level music students and scholarship recipients; they are paid by the foundation). Volunteer opportunities include a Women's Council, which helps out on different projects such as mailings and organizing event fund-raisers, and a Business Advisory Board, consisting of professionals who offer their business knowledge on fund-raising and other practical issues.

## HEALTH

**Hospitals** integrate volunteers into a wide range of programs dealing with patients, including admissions, friendly visiting, language translating, help in feeding and other care, assisting in occupational and speech therapy, escorting to and from X-ray and therapy departments, providing reassurance in emergency rooms and waiting rooms, clerical assistance, reception, gift shop sales, and other functions.

**Hospices** and **in-home hospice programs** match terminally ill patients with volunteers who form a relationship of reassurance and caring for the practical and emotional needs of the dying person and his or her family.

Friendly visitors in **nursing homes** bring warmth and a continuity of human caring to people who might otherwise be isolated or ignored.

Many **clinics** use volunteers to receive, prepare, and comfort patients. **Public health programs,** such as flu immunization campaigns and public-education projects, use volunteers in administration and publicity. **Blood banks** are often partially staffed by volunteers. **Visiting nurse services** use volunteers in preparing materials, friendly visiting, and telephone reassurance.

**AIDS groups** have responded to the epidemic by raising money, forming buddy systems to support people with AIDS, advocating for their rights, working to provide them with quality health care and housing, staffing hot lines, and lobbying for aggressive efforts to stop the disease.

**Health organizations** of all kinds work for the cure of, and public education about, specific diseases, and for the support of the victims of those illnesses.

**Alzheimer's Association**
919 North Michigan Avenue, Suite 1000
Chicago, IL 60611
312-335-8700
Web site: http://www.alz.org

The Alzheimer's Association is dedicated to easing the burden of Alzheimer's disease for patients and their families. Some of the association's activities include supporting research into the cause, new treatments, and cure for Alzheimer's; offering patient and family services; providing public education through books, brochures, newsletters, public-service announcements, and other information; advocating on behalf of patients; and sponsoring seminars on Alzheimer's disease. Chapters are staffed largely by volunteers.

**American Cancer Society**
1599 Clifton Road NE
Atlanta, GA 30329
404-320-3333
Web site: http://www.cancer.org

The American Cancer Society is dedicated to saving lives and diminishing suffering from cancer, and also to eliminating cancer as a major health problem. Its programs are wide-ranging, focusing on preventing, diagnosing, detecting, and treating the many forms of cancer. The society also performs and sponsors research; provides public education and outreach; and offers special services to cancer patients. Volunteers are intimately involved at every level of the organization, helping to plan and implement cancer-control programs, raise funds, and create policy.

**American Diabetes Association**
National Center, PO Box 25757
1660 Duke Street
Alexandria, VA 22314
703-549-1500
Web site: http://www.diabetes.org

The ADA is both a professional organization and a private, nonprofit public-service group. It aims to educate the public about the seriousness of diabetes, to involve people in its work to prevent and cure the disease, and to improve the well-being of diabetes sufferers. Through its many state and local chapters, the association funds research; provides services and information to people with diabetes and their families and friends, along with health professionals and scientists; raises funds for its programs; sponsors local support groups; advocates on behalf of diabetics; and helps develop professional guidelines for diabetes treatment.

**American Foundation for the Blind**
15 West 16th Street
New York, NY 10011
212-502-7600
800-232-5463
Web site: http://www.afb.org/afb

The American Foundation for the Blind (AFB), founded in 1921, serves the needs of the blind and visually impaired through public education, social and technological research, recorded books and periodicals, consultations and referrals, consumer products, publications, and advocacy programs. It is the organization to which Helen Keller devoted forty years of her life. AFB works in partnership with more than seven hundred schools, senior-citizen centers, corporations, consumer groups, and professional organizations, and has a wide range of opportunities for volunteers—among them board membership, reading and recording for the blind, consulting, and assisting in the library. Interested volunteers who send a letter of request for information will receive numerous pamphlets on publications, a sheet explaining Braille, and numbers to call to donate time.

**American Heart Association**
7272 Greenville Avenue

Dallas, TX 75231-4596
214-363-6300
Web site: http://www.amhrt.org

The American Heart Association aims to reduce premature death and disability from cardiovascular disease—the nation's number-one killer—and to provide the public with reliable information on preventing and treating heart attack, stroke, and related illness. The scientific research it sponsors has led to important discoveries such as CPR, bypass surgeries, and life-extending drugs. It also provides public and professional education, including brochures, public-service announcements, and kits that tell how to reduce the risk of heart disease; sponsors community-service programs to help people stop smoking and improve their diet; and offers employee wellness programs and CPR training. Fund-raising is also a major activity, as the association is run on private donations.

**American Lung Association**
1740 Broadway
New York, NY 10019
212-315-8700
Web site: http://www.lungusa.org

The American Lung Association and its medical arm, the American Thoracic Society, are dedicated to controlling and preventing all lung diseases and some of their related causes, including smoking, air pollution, and workplace hazards. The association works with other organizations to perform community service; offers public, professional, and patient education and research; and makes policy recommendations regarding medical care of lung diseases. ALA's programs are partly supported by donations to Christmas Seals. Volunteer opportunities include serving as officers and members of boards of directors, helping to plan and conduct program activities, and assisting with fund-raising.

**Arthritis Foundation**
1330 West Peachtree Street
Atlanta, GA 30309
404-872-7100
Web site: http://www.arthritis.org

The Arthritis Foundation aims to find the cause and cures for the more than 100 forms of arthritis, and to improve the quality of life for the nation's forty million arthritis sufferers. The foundation supports direct research on arthritis and the training of research scientists; it funds clinical research centers, patient services programs, and other educational and advocacy activities on behalf of arthritis. It also offers a large number of community-based services nationwide, including an information service to answer questions from the public, self-help courses, exercise classes, support groups, home-study courses, educational brochures, and continuing education for medical professionals. Volunteer opportunities include serving on policy and program committees, becoming a trainer or a support-group leader, staffing health-fair booths, acting as a phone buddy, lobbying legislators, recruiting corporate sponsors, or helping to organize "fun" fundraisers, which have included a mini Grand Prix where entrants race tiny cars through city streets.

**Gay Men's Health Crisis**
119 West 24th Street
New York, NY 10011
212-807-6664
Web site: http://www.gmhc.org

GMHC is the nation's oldest and largest nonprofit AIDS organization; it helps treat and care for the needs of men, women, and children with AIDS, and advocates for fair and effective AIDS policies at all levels of government. Each year, it sponsors the now-famous fund- and awareness-raising walk-a-thon, AIDS Walk New York, as well as an AIDS Dance-a-Thon. Some of GMHC's activities include AIDS prevention programs; providing support and therapy groups for people with AIDS and their loved ones; patient recreation services; a "buddy system," in which helpers visit clients at home and assist with household tasks; sending volunteer crisis counselors to work with people with AIDS; and legal, financial, and health-care advocacy services to people with AIDS. GMHC also collects statistics on AIDS, maintains a speakers bureau, and publishes informational brochures.

**Leukemia Society of America**
600 Third Avenue
New York, NY 10016
212-573-8484
Web site: http://www.leukemia.org

The Leukemia Society of America is dedicated to curing leukemia and related cancers, including lymphoma, multiple myeloma, and Hodgkin's disease, and to improving the quality of life for patients and their families. As well, it creates public awareness about these diseases, develops resources for professionals, supports private research, and lobbies for government research funding. Its fifty-eight chapters in thirty-four states and Washington, D.C., offer patient assistance, public and professional education, information, and referrals. Volunteer medical professionals can help train professionals and assist patients; other volunteers are needed to plan and participate in special events, solicit funds, run family support groups, and develop Web sites.

**Muscular Dystrophy Association**
3300 East Sunrise Drive
Tucson, AZ 85718
520-529-2000
Web site: http://www.mdausa.org

The MDA, made famous by the annual Labor Day telethon on behalf of "Jerry's Kids," fosters research into the cause and cure not only for muscular dystrophy, but for dozens of other neuromuscular diseases such as Lou Gehrig's disease, myasthenia gravis, and hyperthyroidism. The MDA supports international research programs by offering more than four hundred research awards; it also sponsors university research and more than two hundred outpatient clinics; provides direct patient services, including diagnostic exams, wheelchairs, physical therapy, summer camps for kids, and more. Volunteers are heavily involved in fund-raising activities and in publicizing the organization's work.

**National Alliance for the Mentally Ill (NAMI)**
2101 Wilson Boulevard, Suite 302
Arlington, VA 22201
703-524-7600
800-959-NAMI
Web site: http://www.nami.org

The National Alliance for the Mentally Ill is a grass-roots, self-help support and advocacy organization of people with mental illness, their families, and friends. Through some one thousand chapters across the nation, it aims to eradicate serious mental illness, such as schizophrenia and manic-depressive illness, and to improve the quality of life for sufferers. Each year, NAMI sponsors Mental Illness Awareness Week. The alliance provides emotional support and information on the biological nature of serious mental illnesses, offers local family-support groups, advocates for better treatment for the mentally ill and access to community services such as housing and rehabilitation, promotes research on causes and treatments for serious mental illness, seeks to eliminate the stigma of these disorders, provides information and referrals, and raises funds from individual donors.

**National Down Syndrome Society**
666 Broadway
New York, NY 10012
212-460-9330
800-221-4602
Web site: http://www.ndss.org

The National Down Syndrome Society works on behalf of individuals with Down syndrome and families with Down syndrome children. It promotes public awareness about Down syndrome, including education on myths and truths about this condition; supports research into its causes and prevention; and seeks answers to the medical, genetic, behavioral, and learning problems associated with Down syndrome. The NDSS also develops programs and services, including a free education packet, an 800 hotline to answer questions and concerns and supply referrals to parent support groups and other resources, and annual "Buddy Walks" staged by local chapters to raise awareness and funds.

**National Easter Seal Society**
280 West Monroe, Suite 1800
Chicago, IL 60606
312-726-6200
Web site: http://www.seals.com

The National Easter Seal Society seeks to meet the needs of people with disabilities and help them reach their highest level of independence. It aims to pass legislation affecting the lives of people with disabilities, and mounts public-education campaigns to encourage positive attitudes toward them. One of its newer programs, Access Science, introduces kids with disabilities and their families to hands-on science activities and to role models working in science, math, and technology fields. Easter Seals' network of chapters in all fifty states and some five hundred service sites provide rehabilitative services to more than one million disabled people each year, including physical, occupational, and speech/language therapies; vocational evaluation and training; camping and recreation; psychological counseling; referrals; and assistive technologies.

**National Multiple Sclerosis Society**
733 Third Avenue, 6th Floor
New York, NY 10017
212-986-3240
Web site: http://www.nmss.org

The National Multiple Sclerosis Society serves people with multiple sclerosis, their families, health professionals, and members of the public interested in MS. The society supports research into the causes and treatments of MS, public education on the disease, and patient advocacy; it also designs programs. Its 140 local chapters provide direct services to MS patients, including counseling and referrals; it has eighty-eight treatment centers in thirty-one states. Volunteers are involved in direct service (providing transportation, running support groups, visiting patients, acting as telephone buddies), as well as working in fund-raising and awareness campaigns.

**Prevent Blindness America**
500 East Remington Road
Schaumburg, IL 60173
847-843-2020
Web site: http://www.preventblindness.org

Formerly the National Society to Prevent Blindness, this organization works to preserve sight and prevent blindness through community-service programs, public and professional education, and research. The society distributes information on eye care and safety, disease prevention, and medical centers that diagnose and treat eye disease; offers community services such as eye exams and self-help groups for people with glaucoma; funds research, including new methods for diagnosing and treating glaucoma; runs educational programs for older adults; and maintains a toll-free information service. Volunteers perform and help run child vision screenings, help in affiliate offices, and serve on boards and committees of the national organization and local organizations across the country.

**Volunteers for Medical Engineering**
2301 Argonne Drive
Baltimore, MD 21218
410-243-7495

VME is a volunteer association of engineers, technicians, and defense-industry professionals who donate their talents to developing and supplying medical technology to solve problems faced by people with disabilities. Examples of past projects include an apparatus designed to help disabled people walk and a computer program that helps aphasia sufferers relearn verbal skills. There are various chapters around the country; the national office provides volunteer training, raises funds, and runs an equipment-loan center and a prototyping center. Some volunteers work directly on technology for specific clients, which includes providing them with advice and training them to use the device invented for them; others serve as short-term consultants or work in management, provide referrals, answer phones, or fulfill speaking engagements. VME also seeks contributions of equipment, such as computers and medical devices.

## ENVIRONMENT/ANIMALS

**Environmental groups** work for the protection of the natural world, advocating against air and water pollution and the destruction of the natural environment. Many support educational and advocacy programs on the local, state, and national levels. Some conduct environmental research projects, run cleanup campaigns, operate educational centers, and rescue injured animals. **Neighborhood cleanup groups** and **recycling centers** are grass-roots efforts for a healthy environment.

**Parks,** municipal, state, and national, often use squads of volunteers as monitoring and cleanup personnel and as trail guides. Some conduct sports and recreation programs.

**Zoos** are sources of education and enjoyment for children and adults. In many large and small zoos, volunteers play roles that range from selling souvenirs in the gift shop to guiding tours to helping care for the animals. Volunteers in **botanical gardens** conduct tours and assist in greenhouse and groundskeeping work.

**Societies for the Prevention of Cruelty to Animals** throughout the country work for the care and protection of animals.

**American Society for the Prevention of Cruelty to Animals
(ASPCA)**
424 East 92nd Street
New York, NY 10128
212-876-7700
Web site: http://www.aspca.org

The ASPCA seeks to prevent cruelty to both pets and wild animals, to promote animal appreciation, and to create and enforce laws to protect animals. The society maintains shelters for lost, stray, and unwanted animals; operates a veterinary hospital and a low-cost spay/neuter clinic; conducts educational programs such as Dog Bite Prevention Week; distributes animal-related information for both schoolchildren and adults, including tips on hot- and cold-weather pet care; operates pet-therapy programs; and offers consulting services. Each year, the ASPCA holds a NYC Dog Walk to raise funds for homeless and abandoned pets; the 1997 theme was "Woofstock." Volunteers also help with adoptions; offer foster care for sick or injured animals; serve as dog walkers for kenneled dogs; write letters to legislators; help write brochures; and more.

**Cincinnati Zoo**
3400 Vine Street
Cincinnati, OH 45220
513-281-4701
Web site: http://www.cincyzoo.org

The Cincinnati Zoo, home of the first "test-tube baby" gorilla, not only has some unusual exhibits and programs, but offers an unusual number of volunteer opportunities. Besides providing a home to scores of animals and plants, it serves as a conservation center, cooperating with worldwide conservation organizations. The zoo is especially committed to working with the endangered Asian elephant and is developing a "Vanishing Giants" elephant exhibit; it also has wildlife education programs, an exotic travel program, and gardening classes. Volunteers can serve as tour guides for schoolchildren; work in the Speakers' Bureau or the Media Center; assist with ADOPT (Animals Depend on People Too), a fundraising plan in which people pledge money to feed a specific zoo animal or plant; perform as Zoosters, a group that hand-makes and sells items at special events, or manage the Zoo Shop, among many other activities.

**Earthwatch**
580 Mount Auburn Street
PO Box 9104

Watertown, MA 02272-9104
617-926-8200
Web site: http://www.earthwatch.org

Earthwatch supports scientific and scholarly research projects around the world in order to expand knowledge of the earth and its inhabitants, preserve endangered species and habitats, and promote international co-operation. Volunteer participants age sixteen and up devote several weeks to serving on research expeditions as part of fieldwork teams, and are expected to donate part of the funding for the project. Locations can be as exotic as Siberia or as nearby as Appalachia; botany, paleontology archaeology, and the study of dolphins are just a few of the sciences Earthwatch expeditions might involve. The organization also offers fellowships to help teachers and students to participate in these projects.

**Greenpeace**
1436 U Street NW
Washington, DC 20009
202-462-1177
Web site: http://www.greenpeaceusa.org

Known for its nonviolent "creative confrontation" tactics, such as hanging banners off buildings or sending its fleet of ships to impede nuclear testing, Greenpeace campaigns for systemic changes on behalf of the environment, public health, and a "greener" future. Some of its major areas of interest are pollution prevention, nuclear disarmament, clean energy, and biodiversity. Recent projects include fighting genetically engineered foods, removing toxic chemicals from children's toys and dry-cleaning processes, and eliminating dioxin in manufacturing. Greenpeace's Climate Change Campaign fights global warming and works to save the atmosphere's ozone layer. Volunteers can get involved with its public education campaigns, community organizing, lobbying, research, litigation, and training and technical assistance. Besides its many chapters across the

United States, Greenpeace has offices and projects taking place all over the world.

### The Humane Society of the United States
2100 L Street NW
Washington, DC 20037
202-452-1100
Web site: http://www.hsus.org

The Humane Society of the United States is the nation's largest animal-protection organization; it fosters respect, understanding, and compassion for all creatures, wild and domestic. One of its top priorities is reducing the number of homeless cats and dogs and the suffering these animals experience. The Humane Society also works to stop the use of live animals for testing and research; to protect marine animals; and to improve conditions for farm animals raised as food. It also offers "humane education" and training seminars to ensure quality care for companion animals; monitors national policies regarding animals; works to secure laws to protect endangered species, fur-bearing animals, wild horses, and whales; and sponsors National Animal Shelter Appreciation Week and Prevent-a-Litter Month.

### The Izaak Walton League of America
707 Conservation Lane
Gaithersburg, MD 20878
301-548-0150
Web site: http://www.iwla.org

The Izaak Walton League is a conservation organization working to protect natural resources on the local, state, and national levels using a commonsense, grass-roots approach. League members are hunters, fishermen, and others who share a commitment to conserve and wisely use the nation's soil, air, waters, woods, and wildlife. The league has hundreds of local chapters, many of which hold property and are involved in conservation and outdoor-recreation activities, including fishing and wildlife habitat clinics, stream-monitoring projects (such as Save Our Streams, a nationwide river conservation program), bird-watching, wildlife photography, programs for young people, tree planting, hunting safety instruction, and environmental education and advocacy. Volunteers are involved in every phase of league efforts.

**Keep America Beautiful**
Washington Square
1010 Washington Boulevard
Stamford, CT 06901
203-323-8987
Web site: http://www.kab.org

Keep America Beautiful is committed to preserving America's natural beauty, environment, and resources, and to improving waste-handling at the community level. A leader in litter prevention, community improvement, and beautification, Keep America Beautiful promotes a structured, community-based program, the KAB system, that helps communities prevent litter and generate systematic waste management. There are now amost five hundred ongoing, certified KAB system programs in more than forty states. Some of its other initiatives include the GLAD Bag-a-thon, a cleanup event, and campaigns to stop graffiti, recycle batteries, and encourage buying recycled materials. Volunteers run educational workshops, special events, litter-prevention programs, and executive planning meetings.

**National Audubon Society**
700 Broadway
New York, NY 10003
212-979-3000
Web site: http://www.audubon.org

The National Audubon Society is a conservation organization that works at every level, from local to international, to conserve and restore natural ecosystems, especially for birds and other wildlife. Programs focus on scientific research, wildlife protection, conservation education, and environmental action, with recent priorities centered on preserving wetlands, reauthorizing the Endangered Species Act, and conserving marine wildlife. The Audubon Society purchases and maintains a system of sanctuaries and nature centers nationwide that protect more than 250,000 acres of unique natural habitat. It also runs education centers, nature workshops for school classrooms, and camps; produces television specials; and publishes *Audubon* magazine. Local chapters sponsor activities such as field trips, films, and lectures.

**The Nature Conservancy**
1815 North Lynn Street
Arlington, VA 22209
703-841-5300
Web site: http://www.tnc.org

The Nature Conservancy is an international organization dedicated to preserving global biological diversity and protecting ecologically significant areas and the animals and plants they support. The organization calls itself "Nature's Real Estate Agent," because of its unique approach: First, it identifies the habitats of rare and endangered species, then buys or leases the lands and manages them as private nature preserves. The conservancy operates the largest such sanctuary system in the world, with more than 1,500 sites. Volunteers work in every capacity, from helping to clear brush to counting birds to answering phones. The conservancy also offers internships and temporary unpaid positions, and runs Adopt-an-Acre and Rescue-a-Reef programs that earmark donated money for certain areas and allow contributors to visit and study the areas they've helped protect.

**Audubon Zoological Gardens**
6500 Magazine Street
New Orleans, LA
504-861-2537
Web site: http://www.auduboninstitute.org

This zoo in New Orleans has been rated as one of the best, both in the South and nationwide. The zoo's fifty-eight acres are home to more than 1,500 of the world's rarest animals displayed in their natural habitats, including Australian koalas and the world's only white alligators. Other exhibits include the Louisiana Swamp, Butterflies in Flight, sea lion shows, a tropical birdhouse, the World of Primates, and more. Members of its Volunteer Corps conduct animal presentations, operate interactive stations, answer visitors' questions, help care for animals, and are involved in conservation and education programs.

**Rainforest Action Network**
221 Pine Street, Suite 500
San Francisco, CA 94104
415-398-4404
Web site: http://www.ran.org

Rainforest Action Network is a nonprofit activist organization working to saving the world's rainforests. In cooperation with other environmental and human rights organizations around the world, it stages major campaigns to protect rainforests and the unique or endangered species that live there, and supports peoples from rainforest cultures who are fighting to gain land title rights. At the heart of the organization are grassroots-level Rainforest Action Groups (RAGs) in communities and on campuses. Their activities include direct action, public education, community organizing, fund-raising, and producing publications. Recent campaigns include the Ancient Redwoods Campaign, which has involved demonstrations and boycotts of products made from old-growth forest woods, and a Protect-an-Acre program.

**Sierra Club**
730 Polk Street
San Francisco, CA 94109
415-776-2211
Web site: http://www.sierraclub.org

The Sierra Club is a nonprofit organization that promotes conservation of the natural environment by influencing public policy decisions through lawful means. Among its missions are "to explore, enjoy, and protect the wild places of the earth; to practice and promote the responsible use of the earth's ecosystems and resources; [and] to educate and enlist humanity to protect and restore the quality of the natural and human environment." The club is also known for its strong involvement in international population and family-planning issues from an environmental perspective. Major campaigns are mounted on specific issues selected by national officials, then implemented by both volunteers and paid professionals. There are several volunteer chapters in every state, which focus on local issues they select. For example, one urban New Jersey chapter worked to prevent a golf course from being built in a state park.

## INTERNATIONAL ORGANIZATIONS

**Secular and religious development** and **relief agencies** send emergency food and nutritional and agricultural advisers to developing countries throughout the world. Others provide short- and long-term medical and other technical aid in the form of supplies and personnel. Through **sponsorship programs,** Americans can send money for the care of a child in a foreign country. Exchange programs promote international understanding.

**AmeriCares Foundation**
161 Cherry Street
New Canaan, CT 06840
203-966-5195
800-486-HELP
Web site: http://www.americares.org

This international nonprofit disaster-relief and humanitarian-aid organization mobilizes immediate responses to the emergency medical and practical needs of people around the world. Working with corporations and various agencies and individuals, it collects donations of surplus goods and directs them specifically where they are needed. AmeriCares also serves in many ways in the United States: The organization runs Camp AmeriKids, a free camp for disadvantaged, severely ill youngsters; it created the Bivvy Project, which makes and distributes sleeping gear for homeless people trapped in winter storms in several major cities; and it runs Homefront, which provides supplies and teams of volunteer workers to help homeowners physically or financial unable to repair their own homes.

**Amnesty International USA**
322 Eighth Avenue
New York, NY 10001

212-807-8400

Web site: http://www.amnesty.org

Amnesty International seeks to end human-rights violations wherever they occur. This worldwide, independent movement seeks the release of political prisoners—people detained for their beliefs, color, sex, ethnic origin, language, or religion who have not used or advocated violence. Amnesty works for fair and prompt trials for these prisoners; it also opposes the death penalty and torture. Focusing on individual cases, it works not against specific nations but on behalf of ending specific atrocities. Amnesty's tactics include community organizing, public education, and producing an annual country-by-country report on the state of human rights. Volunteer "Freedom Writers" based in communities and on college campuses stage letter-writing campaigns on behalf of individual prisoners. Volunteers also help publicize and organize actions on behalf of these prisoners. Other recent campaigns have included ending acts of repression in Kenya and assuring the rights of refugees to sanctuary.

**Food for the Hungry**
7729 East Greenway Road
Scottsdale, Arizona 85260
602-998-3100
Web site: http://www.fh.org

This nondenominational Christian relief and development agency has programs in some dozen countries. Food for the Hungry's two distinctive programs are Hunger Corps and EveryChild. Trained Hunger Corps volunteers—with and without previous experience—raise their own support and serve for anywhere from a few months to two years in Third World countries, sharing their skills. Among many other roles, they help to distribute food, work in horticulture or small-animal husbandry, and teach, and are involved in projects such as building a dam or conducting nutritional surveys. Everychild invites people to "sponsor" a child abroad with a small monthly donation that helps buy food, medical care, and other necessities and helps support the child's family and community with seed, tools, solar cookers, and other self-help items. Recently, a Food for the Hungry project helped returning Rwandan refugees plant their crops.

**Freedom From Hunger (formerly Meals for Millions)**
1644 DaVinci Court
Davis, CA 95617
916-758-6200
Web site: http://www.freefromhunger.org

Freedom From Hunger aims to end hunger by overcoming the root causes of poverty. Operating in rural regions of impoverished countries in Africa, Asia, and Latin America, its unique self-help program, Credit with Education, arms self-employed women with a combination of money and information. By making small loans—on average, just $65—it helps these women to build businesses so they and their families can become healthier, better fed, and better off financially. At the same time as participants repay their loans at weekly meetings, they learn about health, nutrition, family planning, and business management skills from FFH representatives working in their communities.

**International Executive Service Corps**
333 Ludlow Street
Stamford, CT 06902
203-967-6000
Web site: http://www.iesc.org

IESC is a business-development organization in which working and retired senior executives and other highly experienced professionals volunteer to live abroad for short periods to assist and instruct entrepreneurs, commercial enterprises, and nonprofit organizations. The organization offers a broad range of advisory and business services to tens of thousands of clients in scores of nations around the world, helping them to create new businesses and new jobs that bring higher standards of living. Client companies served by IESC have also entered into joint ventures or other alliances with American businesses.

**International Rescue Committee**
122 East 42nd Street
New York, New York 10168
212-551-3000
Web site: http//www.intrescom.org

Over sixty years old, founded at the request of Albert Einstein to assist anti-Nazis fleeing Hitler, the IRC is the leading nonsectarian private voluntary agency assisting refuges worldwide. IRC also assists internally displaced populations within their own borders. Recent missions have included helping victims of the fighting in Yugoslavia, Bosnia, Rwanda, and Tajikistan. IRC's priority is to deliver critical medical services, food, and shelter as well as essential public health and sanitation assistance. Once a crisis is stabilized, IRC establishes programs that enable refugees to cope with life in exile. A recent issue of *U.S. News and World Report* singled out IRC as one of only five "standout good guys."

**Interplast, Inc.**
300-B Pioneer Way
Mountain View, CA 94041
415-962-0123
Web site: http://www.interplast.org

Interplast (short for International Plastic Surgery) is an association of volunteer surgeons, pediatricians, anesthesiologists, nurses, and support people. Interplast programs partner these professionals with medical teams in Third World nations to perform free reconstructive surgery to children and adults with birth defects, severe burns, and other crippling deformities. Volunteer doctors travel to countries including Chile, Cyprus, Honduras, Nepal, and the Philippines; besides performing about 1,500 surgeries each year, they train their international colleagues in medical techniques and help them develop their own treatment resources. Interplast volunteers also serve as goodwill ambassadors to the nations they visit.

**Northwest Medical Teams**
PO Box 10
Portland, OR 97208
513-371-0426
Web site: http://www.nwmti.org

Northwest Medical Teams is a Christian relief agency dedicated to providing medical care, equipment, and supplies to the world's needy through visiting teams of volunteer physicians, nurses, and medical technicians. NMT focuses mainly on emergency relief for natural or man-made disasters, but also provides intermediate care to victims of famine and political refugees, and long-term clinic care for people with acute and infectious diseases. It also trains local doctors and staff, and runs Bible clubs in the communities it serves. In the United States, NMT has established a mobile health-care clinic in Portland that provides checkups, dental care, inoculations, and other services.

**Oxfam America**
26 West Street
Boston, MA 02111
617-482-1211
Web site: http://www.oxfamamerica.org

Oxfam funds development projects and disaster relief for poor and marginalized people in Africa, Asia, Latin America, and the Caribbean. It works both on site, giving assistance to grass-roots projects, and at the government level, aiming to influence development-related policy. Overseas, the organization provides grants and technical support for self-help efforts in villages and rural areas where community-based groups are working to increase food production and economic self-reliance. In the United States, it prepares and distributes educational materials, and speaks out about development and hunger-related issues. One recent success: Oxfam helped local community health-care groups in Tanzania drastically reduce cholera there, and worked closely with the government to devise a national strategy to reduce the country's debt. Oxfam volunteers, among other things, lobby lawmakers and stage fundraising efforts.

**Peace Corps**
1970 K Street NW
Washington, DC 20526
202-606-3886
800-551-2214
Web site: http://www.peacecorps.gov

The Peace Corps, a government-sponsored volunteer organization, helps promote world peace and friendship, assists developing countries to meet their needs for skilled men and women, and promotes mutual understanding between the people of these nations and those of the United States. Volunteers of all ages are the backbone of the Peace Corps; they spend two years helping the people in more than sixty countries to meet their basic needs for health care, food, shelter, and education. Skills are needed in a wide variety of areas, including maternal and child health, family nutrition, freshwater fisheries, agriculture extension, teacher training, math and science education, vocational training, small-business consulting, public administration, natural resource development, forestry, conservation, energy, engineering, special education, and industrial arts.

**Save the Children Federation, Inc.**
54 Wilton Road
Westport, CT 06880
203-221-4000
800-243-5075
Web site: http://www.savethechildren.org

This organization makes a lasting, positive difference in the lives of disadvantaged children in the United States and thirty nations through assistance programs made possible by a pool of money generated by individual or group "sponsors." Each sponsor gives small amounts regularly on behalf of an individual child, with whom they can develop a personal relationship through letters and regular reports on his or her progress. Programs also benefit the child's family and community, and include health and nutrition, education, water and sanitation, and other opportunities to improve their quality of life.

**Sister Cities International**
120 South Payne Street
Alexandria, VA 22314
703-836-3535
Web site: http://www.sister-cities.org

The self-described "world's premier citizen diplomacy network," Sister Cities International is the umbrella organization for the Sister Cities program that was launched in 1956 when President Eisenhower called for massive exchanges between Americans and the peoples of other lands. Hundreds of American cities have been paired with a "sister city" abroad; together, citizens and organizations from both communities carry out meaningful exchanges—educational, cultural, technical, and personal— and engage in projects of mutual interest. For example, Louisville, Kentucky, has worked with Perm, Russia, in SCI's Municipal and Community

Problem Solving Program, which mobilizes sister-city partners from the United States and the former Soviet bloc to improve municipal services and solve community problems, such as law enforcement, city planning, and care for the elderly.

**Volunteers in Technical Assistance**
1600 Wilson Boulevard, Suite 500
Arlington, VA 22209
703-276-1800
Web site: http://www.vita.org

Volunteers in Technical Assistance (VITA) is an international development organization that supplies individuals and groups in developing countries with information and technical resources they need to foster self-sufficiency. Its main focuses are agriculture and food processing, renewable energy, water supply and sanitation, housing and construction, and small-business development. Thousands of volunteer technical experts perform needs assessment, assist with program development, offer consulting services and information-systems training, and management for long-term field projects. Recent projects have taken place in African countries, including Madagascar, Chad, and Guinea.

**Youth for Understanding International Exchange**
3501 Newark Street NW
Washington, DC 20016-3167
1-800-TEENAGE
Web site: http://www.yfu.org

YFU is dedicated to improving international and intercultural understanding through exchange programs for high school students. It operates exchange programs with dozens of countries, operating from an International Center in Washington, D.C., and thirteen regional offices across the

United States. Volunteers work with the YFU program in their home communities, helping to recruit and select students and assist with student and host-parent orientation. Volunteers also assist in counseling and support services for exchange students, train other volunteers, and help with fundraising and public affairs.

## GROUPS OF INTEREST TO CHILDREN AND YOUTH

While the following organizations listed below are designed for youth participation, they welcome adults who enjoy working with the young as a mentor, a leader, or a teacher.

**Boy Scouts of America**
1325 West Walnut Hill Lane
Irving, TX 75038
214-580-2000
Web site: http://www.bsa.scouting.org

BSA provides an educational program for boys and young adults (from first-grade Tiger Cubs to teenage Explorers) that helps them build character and develop personal fitness, and trains them in responsible citizenship while they have fun camping, earning merit badges, and attending jamborees, among other activities. Community organizations such as civic groups and churches are granted charters to use scouting as part of their youth programs; they select adult leaders, provide resources and facilities, and recruit participants. Adult Boy Scouts volunteers can serve as troop leaders, participate with their sons in scouting activities, help chartered organizations to use scouting programs, train leaders, and plan and run camping trips.

**Camp Fire, Inc.**
4601 Madison Avenue
Kansas City, MO 64112
816-756-1950
Web site: http://www.campfire.org

Camp Fire is a youth agency serving both boys and girls that seeks to "empower youth to make a difference in the world" and improve conditions in society that affect young people. It has programs in five major areas: clubs, camping and environment, self-reliance, youth leadership, and child care. Through a program of informal education, kids learn self-awareness and develop practical and social skills such as decision-making, problem-solving, and respecting others that will help them realize their potential and become caring, responsible individuals. Volunteers may serve as program leaders, local board members, or office staff in one of the hundreds of local councils nationwide.

**Future Homemakers of America**
1910 Association Drive
Reston, VA 22091
703-476-4900
Web site: http://www.fhahero.org

A national student organization for both boys and girls in junior and senior high schools, Future Homemakers of America aims to help youth assume active roles in society through education in personal growth, family life, career preparation, and community involvement. Programs include improving skills in money management and financial planning; developing leadership skills for careers in food service, among other fields; a peer education program that focuses on personal self-awareness, nutrition, and fitness; and local projects on AIDS education, teen pregnancy, substance abuse, and family communication.

**Girl Scouts of the USA**
830 Third Avenue
New York, NY 10022
212-852-8000
Web site: http://www.gsusa.org

Open to all girls ages five to seventeen and to adult men and women, the Girl Scouts of the USA helps each girl realize her individual potential through activities such as exploring careers and performing community service. Girl Scouts are introduced to science, the arts, the outdoors, and people to help them grow in skills and self-confidence, have fun, make new friends, and earn meaningful recognition. Adult volunteers can serve as board members, consultants, and troop leaders.

**Junior Achievement**
1 Education Way
Colorado Spring, CO 80906
719-540-8000
Web site: http://www.ja.org

Junior Achievement is the world's largest nonprofit economic education organization, with chapters all over the United States and in almost one hundred countries. Its goal: to educate young people on the value of free enterprise, help them understand business and economics, and prepare them to be workforce ready. In partnership with businesses, JA offers in-school programs for kindergarten through grade twelve, focusing on different elements of economics in each grade. Volunteers from the business world teach topics such as the role of business in the community, career preparation, and international trade. The organization also encourages students to stay in school.

**YMCA of the USA**
101 North Wacker Drive
Chicago, IL 60606
312-977-0031
Web site: http://www.ymca.net

All together, YMCAs make up the largest nonprofit community service organization in America, at the heart of community life in neighborhoods and towns across the nation. "Ys" work to meet the health and social-service needs of almost fifteen million men, women, and children of all ages, abilities, and incomes. Though nonsectarian, it also aims to develop values and behavior consistent with Christian principals. Some of the YMCA's organized activities include health and fitness classes in aerobics and swimming, day camps, child care, teen clubs, substance-abuse programs, family nights, adult-education classes, and more. Volunteer board members set policy and help with fund-raising, among other tasks.

**YWCA of the USA**
350 Fifth Avenue, 3rd Floor, Suite 301
New York, NY 10003
212-630-0504
Web site: http://www.ywca.org

The YWCA is the oldest and largest not-for-profit women's organization in the United States, with chapters in all fifty states; it serves about a million girls, women, and their families. Besides offering the vocational, educational, sports, and personal-development programs usually associated with the "Y," and special services for kids, seniors, and people with special needs, today's YWCA aims to empower women and girls and eliminate racism. Volunteers work in partnership with paid staff on programs such as Week Without Violence, which promotes alternatives to violence in homes, schools, and neighborhoods. The YWCA also offers shelter and services to domestic-abuse victims, female leadership training, and is the nation's largest provider of breast-cancer screening and referral programs.

## GROUPS OF INTEREST TO SENIOR CITIZENS AND RETIRED PEOPLE

While all the organizations mentioned welcome volunteers of all ages, if you're heading toward your later years and are specifically interested in issues pertaining to senior citizens, the following may be right for you.

**Gray Panthers**
2025 Pennsylvania Avenue NW, Suite 821
Washington, DC 20006
202-466-3132
800-280-5362

Gray Panthers is an advocacy and education organization that brings people of all ages together to work for social change. In particular, the Gray Panthers promote an "intergenerational" approach to issues, encourage positive attitudes toward aging, and fight age discrimination and other forms of prejudice. Issues of special interest include national health care, Social Security, nursing-home reform, rights of the disabled, housing, and peace and disarmament. The organization collects and distributes information on aging, provides an information and referral service with resources for older people, and sponsors public seminars to combat myths about the aged. Volunteers work on a variety of campaigns through local chapters, which decide their own agendas and strategies.

**Older Women's League (OWL)**
666 11th Street NW, Suite 700
Washington, DC 20001
202-783-6686

This national organization addresses the special concerns of midlife and older women. OWL's purpose is to propose solutions to the difficult problems women face as they age and to educate and support women as they pursue these solutions. OWL's agenda is focused on issues such as Social Security reform, pension rights, health care in retirement, job opportunities, and caregiver support services. With the exception of a small staff, OWL is an all-volunteer organization. Volunteers work on the board of directors, conduct fund-raising and other support activities, and are involved with issue advocacy.

# Acknowledgments

Writing *The Halo Effect* was such a joy because it brought me into contact with people who never failed to improve my day. Their eyes would light up and their voices become charged with animation as they told me how service to others had enhanced their lives and their careers.

This book would never have happened if not for Bob Asahina, president of Golden Books' trade program. Bob came to me several years ago and basically said, "Let's do a project together." He was key in shaping its concept and introduced me to my outstanding agent, Jan Miller, whose infectious support helped make this book happen. Jan also brought me to Gene Stone, my terrific writing partner, who has been at the heart of this project. Gene himself is a volunteer who makes a difference, and working with him over the course of eighteen months was a true privilege and pleasure.

But most of all, I'm indebted to you, the many people whose stories are at the heart of this book. You are role models, and as servant leaders you are helping to make this country of ours an exceptional place in which to live and raise families. You give hope to the dream. If this book leads more people like you to reach out to others with a helping hand, then together, we've done a good thing.

# ABOUT THE AUTHORS

**John Raynolds'** forty-five year career in business, government, the military, and the not-for-profit sector is a vivid validator of the halo effect. Many of his jobs in the business world came about through contacts and skills garnered in the not-for-profit world. After leaving the U.S. Navy, where he was trained as a frogman, his positions included automobile entrepreneur, overseas government intelligence officer, director of corporate development for Mars, Inc., investment banker, president of a venture capital company, CEO of Outward Bound, CEO of Ward Howell (one of the world's leading executive-search firms), and his current position as CEO of the National Peace Garden Foundation in Washington, D.C.

On the not-for-profit side, besides working as a foster parent, president of his local chapter of the American Red Cross, and chairman of the New Canaan Congregational Church, he serves on the boards of ten not-for-profit organizations, including the Achilles Track Club (where he has run four marathons), the International Executive Service Corps, and the Friends of the Youth, the U.S. arm of the program run by the Duke of Edinburgh.

He holds an honorary J.D. degree, is a frequent speaker on the value of balancing career dedication with volunteer work, and is also an active mountaineer, sailor, and outdoorsman—a veteran of forty-one Outward Bound courses, the latest a Himalayan trek in Bhutan. He lives with his wife, Eileen, in Riverside, Connecticut.

**Gene Stone** spent two years in the Peace Corps in Niger, West Africa, serves on the foundation board of Veritas, a drug-rehabilitation program in New York City, and has worked for many other volunteer organizations. A former editor at the *Los Angeles Times* and *Esquire* magazine, he has written articles and columns for numerous publications and is the author of six books, including *Little Girl Fly Away* (Pocket Books).